ـخيرِاللَّه أَوصَدَّق الكَهنـَة وَالعَـرَافـِين

Establishing Proofs regarding

THE RULE ON THOSE WHO SEEK HELP IN OTHER THAN ALLAH

or those who believe in the Soothsayers and Fortunetellers

By:
His Eminence Sheikh

ABDUL AZIZ BIN ABDULLAH BIN BAZ

DARUSSALAM
GLOBAL LEADER IN ISLAMIC BOOKS

Riyadh • Jeddah • Al-Khobar • Sharjah
Lahore • London • Houston • New York

DARUSSALAM

2nd Edition: January 2003

© Maktaba Dar-us-Salam, 1995

King Fahd National Library Cataloging-in-Publication Data

Ibn Baz, Abdul Aziz bin Abdullah

Establishing proofs regarding the rule on those who seek help in other than Allah or those who believe in the Soothsayers and Fortunetellers.

64p., 14x21 cm   **ISBN 9960-740-12-9**

I-Islam-Apologetic works   II. Polytheism   III. Title

240.B345   1160/14

Legal Deposit no. 1160/14

ISBN 9960-740-12-9

Supervised by:
ABDUL MALIK MUJAHID

K.S.A.
- Riyadh
  Darussalam Showroom:
  Tel 00966-1-4614483 Fax: 4644945
- Jeddah
  Darussalam Showroom:
  Tel: 00966-2-6879254 Fax: 6336270
- Al-Khobar
  Darussalam Showroom:
  Tel: 00966-3-8692900
  Fax: 00966-3-8691551

U.A.E
- Darussalam, Sharjah U.A.E
  Tel: 00971-6-5632623 Fax: 5632624

Pakistan
- Darussalam, 50 Lower Mall, Lahore
  Tel: 0092-42-724 0024 Fax: 7354072
  Rahman Market, Ghazni Street
- Urdu Bazar Lahore
  Tel: 0092-42-7120054 Fax: 7320703

U.S.A
- Darussalam, Houston
  P.O Box: 79194 Tx 772779
  Tel: 001-713-722 0419
  Fax: 001-713-722 0431
  E-mail: sales@dar-us-salam.com
- Darussalam, New York
  572 Atlantic Ave, Brooklyn
  New York-11217, Tel: 001-718-625 5925

U.K
- Darussalam International Publications Ltd.
  226 High Street, Walthamstow,
  London E17 7JH, Tel: 0044-208 520 2666
  Mobile: 0044-794 730 6706
  Fax: 0044-208 521 7645
- Darussalam International Publications Limited
  Regent Park Mosque, 146 Park Road,
  London Nw8 7RG Tel: 0044-207 724 3363

France
- Editions & Librairie Essalam
  135, Bd de Ménilmontant- 75011 Paris
  Tél: 0033-01- 43 38 19 56/ 44 83
  Fax: 0033-01- 43 57 44 31
  E-mail: essalam@essalam.com

Australia
- ICIS: Ground Floor 165-171, Haldon St.
  Lakemba NSW 2195, Australia
  Tel: 00612 9758 4040 Fax: 9758 4030

Malaysia
- E&D Books SDN. BHD.-321 B 3rd Floor,
  Suria Klcc
  Kuala Lumpur City Center 50088
  Tel: 00603-21663433 Fax: 459 72032

Singapore
- Muslim Converts Association of Singapore
  32 Onan Road The Galaxy
  Singapore- 424484
  Tel: 0065-440 6924, 348 8344
  Fax: 440 6724

Sri Lanka
- Darul Kitab 6, Nimal Road, Colombo-4
  Tel: 0094-1-589 038 Fax: 0094-74 722433

Kuwait
- Islam Presentation Committee
  Enlightment Book Shop
  P.O. Box: 1613, Safat 13017 Kuwait
  Tel: 00965-244 7526, Fax: 240 0057

India
- Islamic Dimensions
  56/58 Tandel Street (North)
  Dongri, Mumbai 4000 009,India
  Tel: 0091-22-3736875, Fax: 3730689
  E-mail:sales@IRF.net

South Africa
- Islamic Da'wah Movement (IDM)
  48009 Qualbert 4078 Durban,South Africa
  Tel: 0027-31-304-6883
  Fax: 0027-31-305-1292
  E-mail: idm@ion.co.za

بسم الله الرحمن الرحيم

Publisher's Note

The basis of Islam is Monotheism. Allah sent all the Prophets and Messengers to invite mankind towards the worship of the All-Mighty Allah Alone. The Prophets and Messengers had also warned the human beings against ascribing partners to Allah, which is called polytheism.

Polytheism ruins the good deeds of man, leaving him to be exposed to the Hell-fire in the Hereafter. To be successful in this world and in the Hereafter, it is necessary that one should always keep himself away from the acts of polytheism, which has many aspects.

His Eminence, Sheikh 'Abdul 'Aziz bin Abdullah bin Baz has written three short essays to caution us against the various manifestations of polytheism. We are publishing these essays for the benefit of Muslims so that awareness about polytheism may increase and people may stable their beliefs, deeds and actions according to pure Faith in Allah and in accordance with the Noble Qur'ân and the *Sunna* (traditions of the Noble Prophet صلى الله عليه وسلم).

May Allah grant us the supreme success — *Âmîn.*

Abdul Malik Mujahid
General Manager

In the Name of Allah, the Most Beneficent, the Most Merciful

INTRODUCTION

Praise is to Allah and peace and blessings be on the Prophet of Allah; on his family members; and on all those who proceed on his path.

Since the principle of Oneness of Allah formed the basis of the mission of Muhammad bin Abdullah صلى الله عليه وسلم and since this mission is in fact a continuation of the missions of the Prophets who preceded him as stated by Allah in the Noble Qur'ân:

﴿ وَلَقَدْ بَعَثْنَا فِى كُلِّ أُمَّةٍ رَّسُولًا أَنِ اعْبُدُوا اللَّهَ وَاجْتَنِبُوا الطَّاغُوتَ ﴾

"And verily, We have sent among every *Ummah* (community, nation) a Messenger (proclaiming): 'Worship Allah (Alone), and avoid (or keep away from) *Tâghût* (all false deities etc.)". (V.16:36),

and since opposition to heresy and falsehood in its various manifestations, formed the core of this Faith, it is a duty on every Muslim to be well informed about his religion and to worship Allah as ordained by the Islâmic *Shari'a*.

The Muslims of the previous generations had a clear concept regarding their religion because all their beliefs, actions and dealings were in accordance with the Noble Qur'ân and the Pure Traditions (*Sunna* — words and deeds of the Prophet صلى الله عليه وسلم).

Later on, most of the Muslims deviated from this Straight

Path - the path of the Book and the Tradition - and fell apart into factions and groups in all matters pertaining to religion as well as politics and the laws regulating their daily lives. As a result, there came into existence heretical innovations, falsehoods, magic and witchcraft. All these things served as easy loopholes for the enemies of Islâm to attack Islâm and its followers.

The *'Ulamâ'* (learned scholars) of Islâm have, in all periods of history, past and present, cautioned us through their writings against these innovations. This booklet entiled "Establishing the proofs regarding the rule on those who seek help in other than Allah or those who believe in soothsayers and fortune-tellers, by His Eminence, Sheikh 'Abdul-'Aziz bin Abdullah bin Baz, consists of three essays:

1. The Regulation governing the seeking of help from the Prophet صلى الله عليه وسلم.

2. The Regulation governing the seeking of help from jinns and Satan and making vows to them.

3. The Regulation regarding worship through certain innovations which are derived from heretical and polytheistic beliefs.

The Presidency of the Directorates of Islâmic Research, *Ifta, Da'wah* and Guidance has the pleasure to place before the reader this booklet as a contribution towards the enlightenment of the English speaking Muslims against heresy and superstition — so that the general appreciation and understanding of Islâm may increase.

May Allah the All-Mighty make this booklet of use to all Muslims; verily Allah Alone grants success. And may peace be upon Muhammad, his Family and his Companions.

In the Name of Allah, the Most Beneficent, the Most Merciful

THE FIRST ESSAY
The Regulation governing the seeking of help from the Prophet صلى الله عليه وسلم

Praise is to Allah and peace and blessings be upon the Prophet of Allah, the members of his Family and his Companions and on all those who proceed on his path. The weekly magazine, *Al-Mujtama'* of Kuwait, had in its issue No. 15 dated 19-4-1390 A.H., published a poem containing invocations to the Prophet صلى الله عليه وسلم and appeals to him to help the *Ummah* (Islâmic community) and to salvage it from mutual disaccord and disagreements. The poem signed by someone called Āmina, ran as follows:

"O Prophet of Allah, come to the rescue of a world caught in the flames of a war, O Prophet of Allah, come to the rescue of the *Ummah*, plunged in the darkness of doubts since long, O Prophet of Allah, come to the rescue of the *Ummah* which has lost sight of its vision in the wilderness of grief ... etc. etc."

And the poem concludes with the following lines:

"O Prophet of Allah, come to the rescue of the *Ummah*, plunged in the darkness of doubt since long. Pray you! Bring speedy victory as you did at the battle of Badr when you called out to the All-Mighty, And lo! Defeat was turned to a Glorious Victory. Verily Allah has soldiers you do not see."

7

Thus the person who wrote this poem cries out to the Prophet صلى الله عليه وسلم beseeching him to rescue the *Ummah* by achieving speedy victory; she forgets or ignores the fact that victory is granted by Allah the All-Mighty Alone and that it is not in the hands of the Prophet صلى الله عليه و سلم nor in the hands of any other creation. Allah the All-Mighty says in the Noble Qur'an:

﴿ وَمَا ٱلنَّصْرُ إِلَّا مِنْ عِندِ ٱللَّهِ ٱلْعَزِيزِ ٱلْحَكِيمِ ﴾

"...And there is no victory except from Allah, the All-Mighty, the All-Wise." (V.3:126).

﴿ إِن يَنصُرْكُمُ ٱللَّهُ فَلَا غَالِبَ لَكُمْ وَإِن يَخْذُلْكُمْ فَمَن ذَا ٱلَّذِى يَنصُرُكُم مِّنۢ بَعْدِهِۦ ﴾

"If Allah helps you, none can overcome you; and if He forsakes you, who is there after Him that can help you?..." (V.3:160).

It has been established by the verses of the Noble Qur'ân and by the consensus of the *Ummah* that Allah the All-Mighty created all human beings so that they may worship Him. He sent the Messengers and revealed the Books to expound the manner of worship and the path of the mission. In this regard, Allah the All-Mighty states in the Noble Qur'ân:

﴿ وَمَا خَلَقْتُ ٱلْجِنَّ وَٱلْإِنسَ إِلَّا لِيَعْبُدُونِ ﴾

"And I (Allah) created not the jinns and men except they should worship Me (Alone)." (V.51:56)

﴿ وَلَقَدْ بَعَثْنَا فِى كُلِّ أُمَّةٍ رَّسُولًا أَنِ ٱعْبُدُوا۟ ٱللَّهَ وَٱجْتَنِبُوا۟ ٱلطَّٰغُوتَ ﴾

"And verily, We have sent among every *Ummah*

(community, nation) a Messenger (proclaiming): 'Worship Allah (Alone), and avoid (or keep away from) *Tâghût...*' " (V.16:36).

﴿ وَمَآ أَرْسَلْنَا مِن قَبْلِكَ مِن رَّسُولٍ إِلَّا نُوحِىٓ إِلَيْهِ أَنَّهُ لَآ إِلَٰهَ إِلَّآ أَنَا۠ فَٱعْبُدُونِ ﴾

"And We did not send any Messenger before you (O Muhammad صلى الله عليه وسلم) but We inspired him (saying): *Lâ ilâha illa Ana* [none has the right to be worshipped but I (Allah)], so worship Me (Alone and none else)". (V.21:25)

﴿ الٓر كِتَٰبٌ أُحْكِمَتْ ءَايَٰتُهُ ثُمَّ فُصِّلَتْ مِن لَّدُنْ حَكِيمٍ خَبِيرٍ ۝ أَلَّا تَعْبُدُوٓا۟ إِلَّا ٱللَّهَ إِنَّنِى لَكُم مِّنْهُ نَذِيرٌ وَبَشِيرٌ ﴾

"*Alif-Lâm-Râ.* [These letters are one of the miracles of the Qur'ân and none but Allah (Alone) knows their meanings]. (This is) a Book, the Verses whereof are perfected (in every sphere of knowledge, etc.), and then explained in detail from One (Allah), Who is All-Wise and Well-Acquainted (with all things). (Saying) worship none but Allah. Verily, I (Muhammad صلى الله عليه وسلم) am unto you from Him a warner and a bringer of glad tidings." (V.11:1, 2)

It is clear from the above verses that Allah the All-Mighty has created human beings and jinns but for one purpose only: to worship Him Alone and not to attribute any partner to Him. And He has said clearly that the Messengers عليهم الصلاة والسلام were sent to call for this worship and to forbid what is contrary to it. The verses of the Noble Qur'ân are clear and categorical in stating that

9

Allah and Allah Alone is to be worshipped. This worship implies Faith in the Oneness of Allah, obedience to Him, compliance of His Commands and abstention from all that has been forbidden by Him. Allah has ordained these tenets in numerous verses:

﴿ وَمَا أُمِرُوٓا۟ إِلَّا لِيَعۡبُدُوا۟ ٱللَّهَ مُخۡلِصِينَ لَهُ ٱلدِّينَ حُنَفَآءَ ﴾

"And they were commanded not, but that they should worship Allah, and worship none but Him Alone (abstaining from ascribing partners to Him)..." (V.98:5)

and

﴿ وَقَضَىٰ رَبُّكَ أَلَّا تَعۡبُدُوٓا۟ إِلَّآ إِيَّاهُ ﴾

"And your Lord has decreed that you worship none but Him..." (V.17:23)

﴿ إِنَّآ أَنزَلۡنَآ إِلَيۡكَ ٱلۡكِتَٰبَ بِٱلۡحَقِّ فَٱعۡبُدِ ٱللَّهَ مُخۡلِصًا لَّهُ ٱلدِّينَ ۝ أَلَا لِلَّهِ ٱلدِّينُ ٱلۡخَالِصُ ﴾

"Verily, We have sent down the Book to you (O Muhammad صلى الله عليه وسلم) in truth: So worship Allah (Alone) by doing religious deeds sincerely for Allah's sake only, and not to show off, and not to set up rivals with Him in worship. Surely, the religion (i.e. the worship and the obedience) is for Allah only..." (V.39:2,3)

The verses dealing on this concept are abundant in the Noble Qur'ân. They all point to the necessity of sincerity in worshipping Allah Alone and to give up worshipping of all others including the Prophets. There is no doubt that Du'â (invocation) is a vital and comprehensive form of worship; it is to be addressed in all sincerity to Allah Alone as Allah the All-Mighty says in the Noble Qur'ân:

$$\text{﴿ فَٱدْعُوا۟ ٱللَّهَ مُخْلِصِينَ لَهُ ٱلدِّينَ وَلَوْ كَرِهَ ٱلْكَـٰفِرُونَ ﴾}$$

"So, call you (O Muhammad صلى الله عليه وسلم and the believers) upon (or invoke) Allah making (your) worship pure for Him (Alone) (by worshipping none but Him and by doing religious deeds sincerely for Allah's sake only and not to show off and not to set up rivals with Him in worship). However much the disbelievers (in the Oneness of Allah) may hate (it)." (V.40:14)

and

$$\text{﴿ وَأَنَّ ٱلْمَسَـٰجِدَ لِلَّهِ فَلَا تَدْعُوا۟ مَعَ ٱللَّهِ أَحَدًا ﴾}$$

"And the mosques are for Allah (Alone), so invoke not anyone along with Allah." (V.72:18).

This applies to all the creations including the Prophets عليهم السلام because the word *Ahad* in Arabic is indefinite noun used in the context of total negation. Therefore, it applies to all except Allah the All-Mighty.

Allah the All-Mighty says:

$$\text{﴿ وَلَا تَدْعُ مِن دُونِ ٱللَّهِ مَا لَا يَنفَعُكَ وَلَا يَضُرُّكَ ﴾}$$

"And invoke not besides Allah, any that will neither profit you, nor hurt you..." (V.10:106)

This verse is addressed to the Prophet صلى الله عليه وسلم. Needless to say, the Prophet صلى الله عليه وسلم enjoys Divine protection from polytheistic beliefs; the purpose of this verse is to caution others. The All-Mighty says:

$$\text{﴿ فَإِن فَعَلْتَ فَإِنَّكَ إِذًا مِّنَ ٱلظَّـٰلِمِينَ ﴾}$$

"...if (in case) you did so, you shall certainly be one

11

of the *Zâlimûn* (polytheists and wrong-doers)."
(V.10:106).

Thus, the foremost among the mankind, namely the Prophet صلى الله عليه وسلم has himself been cautioned that if he invokes anyone other than Allah, he shall be deemed as one who does wrong. What to say of other human beings?

It must be noted that the word *Zulm* (wrongdoing) is used in the sense of major *Shirk* that is polytheism. Allah the All-Mighty says:

$$ وَٱلْكَٰفِرُونَ هُمُ ٱلظَّٰلِمُونَ $$

"...And it is the disbelievers who are the *Zâlimûn* (wrong-doers, etc.)." (V.2:254)

and

$$ إِنَّ ٱلشِّرْكَ لَظُلْمٌ عَظِيمٌ $$

"... Verily! Joining others in worship with Allah is a great *Zûlm* (wrong) indeed." (V.31:13).

It is evident from all these verses that invocation to anyone other than Allah, whether they be from the dead or trees or idols, etc., is an act of joining others with Allah in worship; it contradicts the purpose of worship for which Allah has created the human beings and the jinns and had sent Prophets عليهم السلام and had revealed the Divine Messages so that they convey the Messages to the people and call them to act upon it. This is the meaning of the phrase 'there is no god except Allah', this statement affirms that there is nothing to be worshipped except Allah the All-Mighty. It is stated in the Noble Qur'ân:

$$ ذَٰلِكَ بِأَنَّ ٱللَّهَ هُوَ ٱلْحَقُّ وَأَنَّ مَا يَدْعُونَ مِن دُونِهِ ٱلْبَٰطِلُ $$

"That is because Allah, He is the Truth, and that

which they invoke besides Him is *Al-Bâtil* (the falsehood, Satan and all other false deities)..." (V.31:30)

This is the essence of religion, and the basic principle of our Faith; no worship will be true unless this principle is truly accepted. Allah the All-Mighty says in the Noble Qur'ân:

﴿ وَلَقَدْ أُوحِىَ إِلَيْكَ وَإِلَى ٱلَّذِينَ مِن قَبْلِكَ لَئِنْ أَشْرَكْتَ لَيَحْبَطَنَّ عَمَلُكَ وَلَتَكُونَنَّ مِنَ ٱلْخَٰسِرِينَ ﴾

"And indeed it has been revealed to you (O Muhammad صلى الله عليه وسلم), as it was to those (Allah's Messengers) before you: 'If you join others in worship with Allah, (then) surely (all) your deeds will be in vain, and you will certainly be among the losers.' " (V.39:65)

and

﴿ وَلَوْ أَشْرَكُوا۟ لَحَبِطَ عَنْهُم مَّا كَانُوا۟ يَعْمَلُونَ ﴾

"...But if they had joined in worship others with Allah, all that they used to do would have been of no benefit to them." (V.6:88).

The religion of Islâm is based on two great principles:

1. That Allah Alone is to be worshipped.

2. That the worship should be according to the path shown by the Prophet of Allah, Muhammad صلى الله عليه وسلم.

This is the meaning of the *Shahâdah* i.e. the Statement of Faith: "There is no god except Allah and that Muhammad is the Messenger of Allah." Therefore, it will be a contradiction of this principle if anyone invokes the dead including the Prophets or others or invokes idols, trees and stones, etc. and seeks their help or seeks to gain favour from them by offering sacrifices of animals or vows or praise for them or prostrates to them.. It will be an act of associating others as Lords of the creation besides Allah the All-Mighty; it will also amount to setting up of rivals to Allah the All-Mighty. In other words, it will be a negation of this basic tenet. It must also be mentioned that anyone who introduces into religion something which has not been permitted by Allah the All-Mighty will be failing to abide by the meaning of the *Shahâdah* that "Muhammad is the Messenger of Allah." Allah the All-Mighty says:

$$﴿ وَقَدِمْنَآ إِلَىٰ مَا عَمِلُوا مِنْ عَمَلٍ فَجَعَلْنَـٰهُ هَبَآءً مَّنثُورًا ﴾$$

"And We shall turn to whatever deeds they (disbelievers, polytheists, sinners etc.) did, and We shall make such deeds as scattered floating particles of dust." (V.25:23).

The deeds referred to here, are the deeds of those who spent their lives in polytheistic beliefs.

In this category of deeds are also included all contrived actions which have not been permitted by Allah; these actions will, on the Day of Judgement, be like floating dust scattered about because it was not in accordance with the Divine Guidance. Prophet Muhammad صلى الله عليه وسلم has said in an authentic *Hadîth* (tradition):

$$«مَنْ أَحْدَثَ فِيْ أَمْرِنَا هٰذَا مَا لَيْسَ مِنْهُ فَهُوَ رَدٌّ»$$

"He who innovates something in this matter of ours that is not of it will have it rejected."

14

The above referred lady writer has addressed an invocation to the Prophet صلى الله عليه وسلم and calls for his help. She has turned away from the Lord of the creations in Whose Hand there is victory as well as defeat, Who Alone bestows help or loss or benefit; none other can benefit nor bestow any such thing. No doubt such an action is a serious violation and it is a *Shirk* (polytheism), the consequences of which will be very grave. Allah the All-Mighty has commanded us to invoke Him and to seek His help; He has promised to respond and He has also threatened with dire consequences to all those who are haughty. He says:

﴿ وَقَالَ رَبُّكُمُ ٱدْعُونِىٓ أَسْتَجِبْ لَكُمْ إِنَّ ٱلَّذِينَ يَسْتَكْبِرُونَ عَنْ عِبَادَتِى سَيَدْخُلُونَ جَهَنَّمَ دَاخِرِينَ ﴾

"And your Lord said: 'Invoke Me, [i.e. believe in My Oneness (Islamic Monotheism)] (and ask Me for anything) I will respond to your (invocation). Verily! Those who scorn My worship [i.e. do not invoke Me, and do not believe in My Oneness, (Islamic Monotheism)] they will surely enter Hell in humiliation!' " (V.40:60)

This verse points out that invocation is a form of prayer and whoever is haughty, his ultimate place of abode will be Hell. If such is the case with regard to one who has had the audacity to avoid praying to Allah, what will be the condition of a person who invokes other than Allah while Allah the All-Mighty is Omnipotent and Omnipresent? The Noble Qur'ân says:

﴿ وَإِذَا سَأَلَكَ عِبَادِى عَنِّى فَإِنِّى قَرِيبٌ أُجِيبُ دَعْوَةَ ٱلدَّاعِ إِذَا دَعَانِ فَلْيَسْتَجِيبُوا لِى وَلْيُؤْمِنُوا بِى لَعَلَّهُمْ يَرْشُدُونَ ﴾

15

"And when My slaves ask you (O Muhammad صلى الله عليه وسلم) concerning Me, then (answer them), I am indeed near (to them by My Knowledge). I respond to the invocations of the supplicant when he calls on Me (without any mediator or intercessor). So let them obey Me and believe in Me, so that they may be led aright."(V.2:186).

It is narrated in an authentic *Hadîth* (tradition of the Prophet) that the Prophet صلى الله عليه وسلم advised his cousin Abdullah bin Abbâs رضى الله عنهما as follows:

«اِحْفَظِ اللهَ يَحْفَظْكَ اِحْفَظِ اللهَ تَجِدْهُ تِجَاهَكَ إِذَا سَأَلْتَ
فَاسْأَلِ اللهَ وَإِذَا اسْتَعَنْتَ فَاسْتَعِنْ بِاللهِ»

"Remember Allah and He will remember you; remember Allah and you shall find Him in your path; If you ask, ask from Allah; and if you seek help, seek from Allah."

And he also said:

«مَنْ مَاتَ وَهُوَ يَدْعُو للهِ نِدًّا دَخَلَ النَّارَ»

"He, who dies while praying to someone as rival to Allah, the reward for such a person shall be the Fire of Hell." (Narrated by Imâm Bukhâri).

In another *Hadîth* (tradition), the Prophet صلى الله عليه وسلم said in an answer to a query as to which is the greatest sin:

«أَنْ تَجْعَلَ للهِ نِدًّا وَهُوَ خَلَقَكَ»

"To make someone as rival to Allah, Who has created you."

So, anyone who prays to other than Allah, seeks his help or gives offering to him or slaughters an animal or offers a

16

prayer to him will be adopting someone as rival to Allah, whether he be a Prophet or a devout person or a king or jinn or an idol or anything else. As regards, invocation to a person who is alive and present before you, it is not an act of *Shirk* (polytheism) because it is quite normal to seek the help of those around you in matters pertaining to the material life to the possible extent; it is a normal and sanctioned practice among Muslims. Allah the All-Mighty says in the Noble Qur'ân in the story pertaining to Moses:

﴿ فَٱسْتَغَٰثَهُ ٱلَّذِى مِن شِيعَتِهِۦ عَلَى ٱلَّذِى مِنْ عَدُوِّهِۦ ﴾

"...The man of his (own) party asked him for help against his foe..." (V.28:15).

and in another verse pertaining also to the story of Moses (Musa عليه السلام) Allah the All-Mighty says:

﴿ فَخَرَجَ مِنْهَا خَآئِفًا يَتَرَقَّبُ ﴾

"So he escaped from there, looking about in a state of fear..." (V.28:21).

Man therefore seeks the help of his fellow human beings at times of war or at times of difficulties that occur to him and which require the help of others. Allah ordered his Prophet صلى الله عليه وسلم to convey to the people that he (the Prophet صلى الله عليه وسلم) does not possess for anyone any good nor any harm. The Noble Qur'ân states:

﴿ قُلْ إِنَّمَآ أَدْعُواْ رَبِّى وَلَآ أُشْرِكُ بِهِۦٓ أَحَدًا ۝ قُلْ إِنِّى لَآ أَمْلِكُ لَكُمْ ضَرًّا وَلَا رَشَدًا ﴾

"Say (O Muhammad صلى الله عليه وسلم): 'I invoke only my Lord (Allah Alone), and I associate none as partners along with Him.' Say: 'It is not in my power to

17

cause you harm, or to bring you to the Right Path.' "
(V.72:20,21)

and

﴿ قُل لَّآ أَمْلِكُ لِنَفْسِى نَفْعًا وَلَا ضَرًّا إِلَّا مَا شَآءَ ٱللَّهُ وَلَوْ كُنتُ أَعْلَمُ
ٱلْغَيْبَ لَٱسْتَكْثَرْتُ مِنَ ٱلْخَيْرِ وَمَا مَسَّنِىَ ٱلسُّوٓءُ إِنْ أَنَا۠ إِلَّا نَذِيرٌ وَبَشِيرٌ
لِّقَوْمٍ يُؤْمِنُونَ ﴾

"Say (O Muhammad صلى الله عليه وسلم): I possess no
power of benefit or hurt to myself except as Allah
will. If I had the knowledge of the *Ghaib* (unseen), I
should have secured for myself an abundance of
wealth, and no evil should have touched me. I am
but a warner, and a bringer of glad tidings unto
people who believe." (V.7:188).

The Qur'ânic verses on this concept are many in number.
The Prophet صلى الله عليه وسلم never invoked anyone other than
Allah and he never sought help from anyone other than
Him; he beseeched Allah the All-Mighty during the battle
of Badr and asked Him for victory against the enemy; he
persistently prayed to Him saying, "O Lord, fulfill for me
Your Promise." He kept repeating these words to the
extent that his friend and companion Abû Bakr رضى الله عنه
said: "May it suffice you, O Prophet of Allah; verily Allah
will fulfill His Promise to you." In this context, Allah
revealed the following verse of the Noble Qur'ân:

﴿ إِذْ تَسْتَغِيثُونَ رَبَّكُمْ فَٱسْتَجَابَ لَكُمْ أَنِّى مُمِدُّكُم بِأَلْفٍ مِّنَ
ٱلْمَلَٰٓئِكَةِ مُرْدِفِينَ ٠ وَمَا جَعَلَهُ ٱللَّهُ إِلَّا بُشْرَىٰ وَلِتَطْمَئِنَّ بِهِۦ
قُلُوبُكُمْ وَمَا ٱلنَّصْرُ إِلَّا مِنْ عِندِ ٱللَّهِ إِنَّ ٱللَّهَ عَزِيزٌ حَكِيمٌ ﴾

"(Remember) when you sought help of your Lord and
He answered you (saying): 'I will help you with a

18

thousand of the angels each behind the other (following one another) in succession.' Allah made it only as glad tidings, and that your hearts be at rest therewith. And there is no victory except by the help of Allah. Verily, Allah is All-Mighty, All-Wise." (V.8:9,10).

Thus Allah the All-Mighty reminds them of their call for help and how He responded to them by sending reinforcements of angels to them and that victory is not from the angels, but the angels were sent only to convey the good news of victory and contentment. Allah says:

$$ ﴿ وَمَا ٱلنَّصْرُ إِلَّا مِنْ عِندِ ٱللَّهِ ﴾ $$

"...And there is no victory except from Allah." (V.3:126)

and

$$ ﴿ وَلَقَدْ نَصَرَكُمُ ٱللَّهُ بِبَدْرٍ وَأَنتُمْ أَذِلَّةٌ فَٱتَّقُوا۟ ٱللَّهَ لَعَلَّكُمْ تَشْكُرُونَ ﴾ $$

"And Allah has already made you victorious at Badr, when you were a weak little force. So fear Allah much (abstain from all kinds of sins and evil deeds which He has forbidden and love Allah much, perform all kinds of good deeds which He has ordained) that you may be grateful." (V.3:123).

Thus Allah granted help at the battle of Badr; the weapons, the power to fight and the angels were all the factors that brought victory and glad tidings. They were only the means by which the Divine victory was granted; victory is therefore from Allah only. So how could the lady writer referred to above or anyone else seek help and victory from the Prophet صلى الله عليه وسلم and turn away from the Lord of all creations Who is Omnipresent and Omnipotent?

No doubt, this attitude only betrays ignorance in its worst forms and indeed it is a major act of *Shirk* (polytheism).

It is therefore a duty on the writer to repent to Allah in all sincerity and to never repeat such a mistake. Sincere repentance requires total conviction and compliance to what has been ordained by Allah. And if the repentance is with regard to the rights of any fellow human beings, such rights should be returned to whom they belong or he (the repentant) should obtain an acquital thereof. Allah has ordered His worshippers to repent and He has promised acceptance of their repentance. He says in the Noble Qur'ân:

﴿ وَتُوبُوٓا۟ إِلَى ٱللَّهِ جَمِيعًا أَيُّهَ ٱلْمُؤْمِنُونَ لَعَلَّكُمْ تُفْلِحُونَ ﴾

"....And all of you beg Allah to forgive you all, O believers, that you may be successful." (V.24:31)

and Allah says with regard to the Christians:

﴿ أَفَلَا يَتُوبُونَ إِلَى ٱللَّهِ وَيَسْتَغْفِرُونَهُۥ وَٱللَّهُ غَفُورٌ رَّحِيمٌ ﴾

"Will they not repent to Allah and ask His Forgiveness? For Allah is Oft- Forgiving, Most Merciful" (V.5:74)

and Allah says:

﴿ وَٱلَّذِينَ لَا يَدْعُونَ مَعَ ٱللَّهِ إِلَٰهًا ءَاخَرَ وَلَا يَقْتُلُونَ ٱلنَّفْسَ ٱلَّتِى حَرَّمَ ٱللَّهُ إِلَّا بِٱلْحَقِّ وَلَا يَزْنُونَ وَمَن يَفْعَلْ ذَٰلِكَ يَلْقَ أَثَامًا ۝ يُضَٰعَفْ لَهُ ٱلْعَذَابُ يَوْمَ ٱلْقِيَٰمَةِ وَيَخْلُدْ فِيهِۦ مُهَانًا ۝ إِلَّا مَن تَابَ وَءَامَنَ وَعَمِلَ عَمَلًا صَٰلِحًا فَأُو۟لَٰٓئِكَ يُبَدِّلُ ٱللَّهُ سَيِّـَٔاتِهِمْ حَسَنَٰتٍ وَكَانَ ٱللَّهُ غَفُورًا رَّحِيمًا ﴾

"And those who invoke not any other *Ilâh* (god)

20

along with Allah, nor kill such life as Allah has forbidden, except for just cause, nor commit illegal sexual inter-course — and whoever does this shall receive the punishment. The torment will be doubled to him on the Day of Resurrection, and he will abide therein in disgrace; Except those who repent and believe (in Islamic Monotheism), and do righteous deeds, for those, Allah will change their sins into good deeds, and Allah is Oft-Forgiving, Most Merciful." (V.25:68-70)

and Allah says:

$$ \text{﴿ وَهُوَ ٱلَّذِى يَقْبَلُ ٱلتَّوْبَةَ عَنْ عِبَادِهِۦ وَيَعْفُوا۟ عَنِ ٱلسَّيِّئَاتِ وَيَعْلَمُ مَا نَفْعَلُونَ ﴾} $$

"And He it is Who accepts repentance from His slaves, and forgives sins, and He knows what you do." (V.42:25).

The Prophet صلى الله عليه وسلم has said:

«الإِسْلَامُ يَهْدِمُ مَا كَانَ قَبْلَهُ وَالتَّوْبَةُ تَجُبُّ مَا كَانَ قَبْلَهَا»

"Islâm obliterates all that has preceded it; and repentance erases all the earlier (wrong) actions."

In this brief essay, I have sought to explain the magnitude and danger of the sin of *Shirk* (polytheism) because it is one of the major sins. It is my earnest desire that the readers should understand the issue in its right perspective and should not be misled by such writers.

In conclusion, I pray to Allah the All-Mighty to make these few words of use to Muslims and may He reform us all and make us proceed always on the right path and fortify us with the knowledge of religion and steadfastness in adhering to it. May Allah protect us from the evils of ourselves and from our bad actions. Verily He is the Protector and Sustainer. Peace and blessings of Allah be upon His slave and Messenger Muhammad and the members of his Family and his Companions.

In the Name of Allah, the Most Beneficent, the Most Merciful

THE SECOND ESSAY
The Regulation governing the seeking of help from jinns and Satan and making vows to them.

From 'Abdul 'Aziz bin Abdullah bin Baz to those Muslims — may Allah bless them and me — who adhere to the religion of Allah and remain committed to it. *Amin.*

May peace, mercy and blessings of Allah be upon you all.

Some friends sought to know from me about the actions of some uninformed brethren of our religion. They stated that these people, at times of calamities, invoke certain forces and seek their help; they invoke for instance, the jinns and give offerings and sacrifices of animals to them; some of them cry out saying, "O you Seven take him!", meaning thereby seven chiefs of the jinns. They might also say, "O you Seven inflict on him such and such things ... break his bones, drink his blood, mutilate his body." Some of them may say, "O the jinn of noon time, O the jinn of *Asr* (evening) time, take him". Such practices are prevalent in some of the southern areas. In addition to those, there is also the invoking of the dead, including the Prophets, the noble souls and angels and others. They are invoked and their help is sought, unfortunately, by many who profess the Faith of Islâm. They do so due to ignorance and due to the desire to imitate and follow what was practised by their forefathers; some of them may justify their actions by saying, "This is something in vogue, we do not mean anything by it nor do we have any faith in it." Some friends also sought my opinion on having relationships of marriage with people known for such actions and on accepting their offerings; offering prayers for them, praying behind them and about belief in magicians and soothsayers who, I was told, claim knowledge of the sickness of a person and the reasons of the sickness by merely casting a look at anything on the body of the patient such as a turban, pyjamas, veil, etc.

In answer to the above, I wish to state the following:-
Praise is to Allah, the One and Only Allah and blessings and peace upon the Prophet of Allah, who was the last of all Prophets; peace and blessings also upon his Family, his Companions and on all those who will abide by the path of right guidance until the Day of Judgement.

Verily Allah the All-Mighty has created the human beings and the jinns in order to worship Him Alone and to abstain from worshipping, invoking, seeking the help and giving offerings and sacrifices and to offer all other worships to none other than Him. Allah has sent the Messengers to guide the people to this task and He revealed the Heavenly Books, the greatest of which is the Noble Qur'ân. It was revealed in order to convey this Message and to preach and to work for it besides cautioning the people against *Shirk* (polytheism) with Allah and against the worshipping of anyone other than Him. This is the purport of the Statement of Faith: "There is no god except Allah"; it clearly sets out the principle that there is no one else to be worshipped except Allah; thus it negates the concept of Godliness to anyone other than Allah; it affirms that Allah Alone and none other than Allah is to be worshipped. There are ample evidences on this in the Noble Qur'ân and in the *Ahâdith* (traditions) of the Prophet صلى الله عليه وسلم.
Allah says in the Noble Qur'ân:

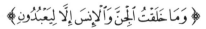
﴿ وَمَا خَلَقْتُ ٱلْجِنَّ وَٱلْإِنسَ إِلَّا لِيَعْبُدُونِ ﴾

"And I (Allah) created not the jinns and men except they should worship Me (Alone)." (V.51:56)

and

$$ \text{﴿ وَقَضَىٰ رَبُّكَ أَلَّا تَعْبُدُوٓا۟ إِلَّآ إِيَّاهُ ﴾} $$

"And your Lord has decreed that you worship none but Him..." (V.17:23)

and

$$ \text{﴿ وَمَآ أُمِرُوٓا۟ إِلَّا لِيَعْبُدُوا۟ ٱللَّهَ مُخْلِصِينَ لَهُ ٱلدِّينَ حُنَفَآءَ ﴾} $$

"And they were commanded not, but that they should worship Allah, and worship none but Him Alone (abstaining from ascribing partners to Him)..." (V.98:5)

and

$$ \text{﴿ وَقَالَ رَبُّكُمُ ٱدْعُونِىٓ أَسْتَجِبْ لَكُمْ إِنَّ ٱلَّذِينَ يَسْتَكْبِرُونَ عَنْ عِبَادَتِى سَيَدْخُلُونَ جَهَنَّمَ دَاخِرِينَ ﴾} $$

"And your Lord said: Invoke Me, [i.e. believe in My Oneness (Islamic Monotheism)] (and ask Me for anything) I will respond to your (invocation). Verily! Those who scorn My worship [i.e. do not invoke Me, and do not believe in My Oneness, (Islamic Monotheism)] they will surely enter Hell in humiliation!" (V.40:60)

and

$$ \text{﴿ وَإِذَا سَأَلَكَ عِبَادِى عَنِّى فَإِنِّى قَرِيبٌ أُجِيبُ دَعْوَةَ ٱلدَّاعِ إِذَا دَعَانِ ﴾} $$

"And when My slaves ask you (O Muhammad صلى الله عليه وسلم) concerning Me, then (answer them), I am indeed near (to them by My Knowledge). I respond to the invocations of the supplicant when he calls on

25

Me (without any mediator or intercessor)..."
(V.2:186)

It is clear from the above verses that the human beings and jinns have been created by Allah in order to worship Him and He has ordained that none other than He be worshipped. The Divine Commandment has been conveyed in the Noble Qur'ân and through the Prophets عليهم السلام that people should worship the One and Only Allah and that invocation to Allah is an important form of worship; whoever is too arrogant to offer this worship shall be doomed to the Fire of Hell. Allah also says in the Noble Qur'ân that:

﴿ وَإِذَا سَأَلَكَ عِبَادِى عَنِّى فَإِنِّى قَرِيبٌ أُجِيبُ دَعْوَةَ ٱلدَّاعِ إِذَا دَعَانِ ﴾

"And when My slaves ask you (O Muhammad صلى الله عليه وسلم) concerning Me, then (answer them), I am indeed near (to them by My Knowledge). I respond to the invocations of the supplicant when he calls on Me (without any mediator or intercessor)..."
(V.2:186)

Hence, it is a duty on all the worshippers to invoke Allah, the One and Only God because such invocation is a form of worship for which they have been created and commanded to act upon. The Noble Qur'ân says:

﴿ قُلْ إِنَّ صَلَاتِى وَنُسُكِى وَمَحْيَاىَ وَمَمَاتِى لِلَّهِ رَبِّ ٱلْعَٰلَمِينَ ۝ لَا شَرِيكَ لَهُۥ وَبِذَٰلِكَ أُمِرْتُ وَأَنَا۠ أَوَّلُ ٱلْمُسْلِمِينَ ﴾

"Say (O Muhammad صلى الله عليه وسلم): Verily, my prayer, my sacrifice, my living, and my dying are for Allah, the Lord of the 'Âlamîn (mankind, jinns and all that exists). He has no partner. And of this I have been

commanded, and I am the first of the Muslims."
(V.6:162,163).

Allah has ordered His Prophet صلى الله عليه وسلم to inform the
people that his prayer and service of sacrifice and life and
death are all for Allah, the Lord of all creations, Who has
no partner. The word 'sacrifice' here refers to the offering
of animal as sacrifice; so if anyone offers a sacrifice to
other than Allah, he then commits an act of *Shirk*, that is
associating someone else with Allah.

It would be like praying to someone else other than Allah
because prayer and sacrifice have equal importance in the
Divine estimation and they are to be for Allah, the One
and Only God. If anyone offers a sacrifice to other than
Allah such as the jinns, the angels, and the dead and others
in an attempt to seek nearness to them, then he is like a
person who prays to other than Allah. The Prophet صلى الله
عليه وسلم has, as per an authentic *Hadith* (tradition) said:

«لَعَنَ اللهُ مَنْ ذَبَحَ لِغَيْرِ اللهِ»

"Curse of Allah be upon those who offer sacrifice to
other than Allah."

Imâm Ahmad has, on the authority of Tariq bin Shihab,
narrated that the Prophet صلى الله عليه وسلم had said:

«مَرَّ رَجُلَانِ عَلَى قَوْمٍ لَهُمْ صَنَمٌ لَا يَجُوزُهُ أَحَدٌ حَتَّى يُقَرِّبَ
لَهُ شَيْئًا فَقَالُوا لِأَحَدِهِمَا قَرِّبْ قَالَ لَيْسَ عِنْدِي شَيْءٌ أُقَرِّبُ
قَالُوا قَرِّبْ وَلَوْ ذُبَابًا فَقَرَّبَ ذُبَابًا فَخَلُّوا سَبِيلَهُ فَدَخَلَ النَّارَ
وَقَالُوا لِلآخَرِ قَرِّبْ قَالَ مَا كُنْتُ لِأُقَرِّبَ لِأَحَدٍ شَيْئًا دُوْنَ اللهِ
عَزَّوَجَلَّ فَضَرَبُوا عُنُقَهُ فَدَخَلَ الْجَنَّةَ»

"Two men passed by a people who had an idol to which an offering had to be made by whoever passed by that idol. The people asked one of the two persons to give some offering, he said, that he had nothing to offer; they told him that he may offer anything, even a small fly; so the man gave a fly as an offering and he was allowed to pass. But his doom was the Fire of Hell. The second person was also asked to do accordingly but that person refused by affirming that he will not give as offering to anyone other than Allah. On his refusal, those people beheaded and killed him, but his ultimate abode was Paradise."

It can be noted from this narration that whoever gives an offering to an idol, though it might be only a fly, will be associating someone else as partner to Allah and therefore deserves punishment in Hell. So what to say of those who invoke the jinns, the angels and the pious people, seeking their help, offering vows to them and trying to gain proximity with them by giving sacrifices of animals to them. The purpose for which one does this is to protect his wealth or cure his illness or the safety of his cattle and his fields; he may also do that out of fear of the jinns. Such people become more deserving of torture in the Hell than that person who killed a fly as an offering to the idol. The Noble Qur'ân says:

﴿ إِنَّآ أَنزَلْنَآ إِلَيْكَ ٱلْكِتَٰبَ بِٱلْحَقِّ فَٱعْبُدِ ٱللَّهَ مُخْلِصًا لَّهُ ٱلدِّينَ ۝ أَلَا لِلَّهِ ٱلدِّينُ ٱلْخَالِصُ ۚ وَٱلَّذِينَ ٱتَّخَذُوا۟ مِن دُونِهِۦٓ أَوْلِيَآءَ مَا نَعْبُدُهُمْ إِلَّا لِيُقَرِّبُونَآ إِلَى ٱللَّهِ زُلْفَىٰٓ إِنَّ ٱللَّهَ يَحْكُمُ بَيْنَهُمْ فِى مَا هُمْ فِيهِ يَخْتَلِفُونَ ۗ إِنَّ ٱللَّهَ لَا يَهْدِى مَنْ هُوَ كَٰذِبٌ كَفَّارٌ ﴾

"Verily, We have sent down the Book to you (O

Muhammad صلى الله عليه وسلم) in truth: So worship Allah (Alone) by doing religious deeds sincerely for Allah's sake only, and not to show off, and not to set up rivals with Him in worship. Surely, the religion (i.e. the worship and the obedience) is for Allah only. And those who take *'Auliyâ'* (protectors and helpers) besides Him (say): 'We worship them only that they may bring us near to Allah.' Verily, Allah will judge between them concerning that wherein they differ. Truly, Allah guides not him who is a liar, and a disbeliever." (V.39:2,3).

and

﴿ وَيَعْبُدُونَ مِن دُونِ ٱللَّهِ مَا لَا يَضُرُّهُمْ وَلَا يَنفَعُهُمْ وَيَقُولُونَ هَـٰٓؤُلَآءِ شُفَعَـٰٓؤُنَا عِندَ ٱللَّهِ قُلْ أَتُنَبِّـُٔونَ ٱللَّهَ بِمَا لَا يَعْلَمُ فِى ٱلسَّمَـٰوَٰتِ وَلَا فِى ٱلْأَرْضِ سُبْحَـٰنَهُۥ وَتَعَـٰلَىٰ عَمَّا يُشْرِكُونَ ﴾

"And they worship besides Allah things that hurt them not, nor profit them, and they say: 'These are our intercessors with Allah.' Say: 'Do you inform Allah of that which He knows not in the heavens and on the earth?' Glorified and Exalted be He above all that which they associate as partners with Him!" (V.10:18).

We learn from the above two verses that the polytheists had taken in lieu of Allah, some creations as their friends and protectors; they worshipped them and invoked them in awe and reverence and offered sacrifice and vows under the assumption that those friends and protectors act as intercessors and take them nearer to Allah. Allah the All-Mighty has proved their falsehood and has described them as liars, infidels, and polytheists; and Allah pre-eminently transcended above the cult of polytheism. The

Noble Qur'ân states:

﴿ سُبْحَـٰنَهُۥ وَتَعَـٰلَىٰ عَمَّا يُشْرِكُونَ ﴾

"...Glorified and Exalted be He above all that which they associate as partners with Him!" (V.10:18).

It is thus clear that whoever takes a king or a Prophet or a jinn or a stone or a tree for the purpose of invocation along with Allah and seeks their help or tries to gain nearness to them by offering vows and sacrifices in the hope that they may intercede with Allah on his behalf, or in the hope of getting cured from some illness, or of safeguarding of wealth or safety for a person who is away or for any other purpose, commits the major crime of *Shirk* (polytheism) regarding which Allah states:

﴿ إِنَّ ٱللَّهَ لَا يَغْفِرُ أَن يُشْرَكَ بِهِۦ وَيَغْفِرُ مَا دُونَ ذَٰلِكَ لِمَن يَشَآءُ وَمَن يُشْرِكْ بِٱللَّهِ فَقَدِ ٱفْتَرَىٰ إِثْمًا عَظِيمًا ﴾

"Verily, Allah forgives not that partners should be set up with Him in worship, but He forgives except that (anything else) to whom He pleases, and whoever sets up partners with Allah in worship, he has indeed invented a tremendous sin." (V.4:48)

and

﴿ إِنَّهُۥ مَن يُشْرِكْ بِٱللَّهِ فَقَدْ حَرَّمَ ٱللَّهُ عَلَيْهِ ٱلْجَنَّةَ وَمَأْوَىٰهُ ٱلنَّارُ وَمَا لِلظَّـٰلِمِينَ مِنْ أَنصَارٍ ﴾

"Verily, whosoever sets up partners in worship with Allah, then Allah has forbidden Paradise for him, and the Fire will be his abode. And for the *Zalimun*

(polytheists and wrong-doers) there are no helpers."
(V.5:72)

On the Day of Judgement intercession will be granted only to the people who believe in the Oneness of Allah and abide by it sincerely; it will   not be granted to the polytheists as stated by   the Prophet صلى الله عليه وسلم, when he was asked about the people who will be fortunate to enjoy his intercession, he said:

«مَنْ قَالَ لَا إِلٰه إِلَّا اللهُ خَالِصًا مِنْ قَلْبِه»

"Whoever says with all sincerity of his heart that there is no god but Allah only."

The Prophet also said:

«لِكُلِّ نَبِيٍّ دَعْوَةٌ مُسْتَجَابَةٌ فَتَعَجَّلَ كُلُّ نَبِيٍّ دَعْوَتَهُ وَأَنَا اخْتَبَأْتُ دَعْوَتِي شَفَاعَةً لِأُمَّتِي يَوْمَ الْقِيَامَةِ فَهِيَ نَائِلَةٌ إِنْ شَاءَ اللهُ مَنْ مَاتَ مِنْ أُمَّتِي لَا يُشْرِكُ بِاللهِ شَيْئًا»

"Every Prophet has an invocation that will be answered;   and every Prophet hastened in his invocation, but I withheld my invocation so that I may intercede for my people on the Day of Judgement. Allah willing, my invocation will also include those of my nation who died without setting up partners to Allah."

The polytheists of the early period believed in Allah as their Lord, Creator, and Sustainer but they relied on Prophets and friends and protectors, angels, trees and stones, etc. in the hope of gaining their intercession with Allah and nearness to Him as Allah said in the verses quoted above. Allah did not pardon them nor the Prophet صلى الله عليه وسلم.   Indeed Allah   has renounced them and has described them as infidels and polytheists. Allah has also disproved their claim that those gods will intercede for them with Allah and take them nearer to Him, the Prophet صلى الله عليه وسلم has fought battles against them in order to make them worship Allah, the One and Only Allah.

In doing so, the Prophet صلى الله عليه وسلم acted according to the Divine Wish stated in the Noble Qur'ân:

﴿ وَقَٰتِلُوهُمْ حَتَّىٰ لَا تَكُونَ فِتْنَةٌ وَيَكُونَ ٱلدِّينُ كُلُّهُۥ لِلَّهِ ﴾

"And fight them until there is no more *Fitnah* (disbelief and polytheism: i.e. worshipping others besides Allah) and the religion (worship) will all be for Allah Alone (in the whole of the world). (V.8:39).

And the Prophet صلى الله عليه وسلم has said:

«أُمِرْتُ أَنْ أُقَاتِلَ النَّاسَ حَتَّى يَشْهَدُوا أَنْ لَا إِلَهَ إِلَّا اللهُ وَأَنَّ مُحَمَّدًا رَسُوْلُ اللهِ وَيُقِيْمُوا الصَّلَاةَ وَيُؤْتُوا الزَّكَاةَ فَإِذَا فَعَلُوْا ذَلِكَ عَصَمُوْا مِنِّي دِمَاءَهُمْ وَأَمْوَالَهُمْ إِلَّا بِحَقِّ الإِسْلَامِ وَحِسَابُهُمْ عَلَى اللهِ»

"I have been ordered to fight people until they witness that there is no god except Allah and that Muhammad is the Prophet of Allah and perform the prayers, and give the *Zakât* (poor tax); if they do so, they shall enjoy safety from me in their lives and wealth except in what is due to Islâm and they shall be answerable to Allah."

The meaning of the phrase 'until they witness that there is

no god except Allah' in this saying of the Prophet is that
they should worship Allah Only and exclusively. The
polytheists were afraid of the jinns and took refuge in
them. In this context, Allah says in the Noble Qur'ân:

﴿ وَأَنَّهُۥ كَانَ رِجَالٌ مِّنَ ٱلْإِنسِ يَعُوذُونَ بِرِجَالٍ مِّنَ ٱلْجِنِّ فَزَادُوهُمْ رَهَقًا ﴾

"True, there were people among mankind who took
shelter with the persons among the jinns, but they
increased them in folly." (V.72:6).

The commentators of the Noble Qur'ân have interpreted
the words 'increased them in folly' as their being struck
with fear and panic because the jinns feel high and mighty
when they see human beings seeking refuge in them and
so they make themselves (that is the jinns) a greater source
of fear and panic so that these human beings may
increasingly worship them and seek refuge in them. But
Allah has guided the Muslims to seek refuge in Him and
in His Complete Words. Allah says:

﴿ وَإِمَّا يَنزَغَنَّكَ مِنَ ٱلشَّيْطَـٰنِ نَزْغٌ فَٱسْتَعِذْ بِٱللَّهِ إِنَّهُۥ سَمِيعٌ عَلِيمٌ ﴾

"And if an evil whisper comes to you from Satan
then seek refuge with Allah. Verily, He is All-
Hearer, All-Knower." (V.7:200).

and

﴿ قُلْ أَعُوذُ بِرَبِّ ٱلْفَلَقِ ﴾

"Say: I seek refuge with (Allah) the Lord of the day-
break." (V.113:1)

and

﴿ قُلْ أَعُوذُ بِرَبِّ ٱلنَّاسِ ﴾

"Say: I seek refuge with (Allah) the Lord of
mankind." (V.114:1)

It is narrated in an authentic *Hadîth* that the Prophet صلى الله

عليه وسلم has said:

«مَنْ نَزَلَ مَنْزِلاً فَقَالَ أَعُوذُ بِكَلِمَاتِ اللهِ التَّامَّاتِ مِن شَرِّ مَا خَلَقَ لَمْ يَضُرُّهُ شَيْءٌ حَتَّى يَرْتَحِلَ مِنْ مَنْزِلِهِ ذَلِكَ»

"Whoever alights at a place and says, 'I seek refuge in the Complete Words of Allah from the evil that He has created' will not be affected by any harm until his departure from that place."

The person seeking safety and protection of his religion and who wishes to be away from *Shirk* (polytheism) in its major and minor forms will understand from the above quoted verses from the Noble Qur'ân and sayings of the Prophet صلى الله عليه وسلم that devotion to the dead and angels, jinns, etc. and invocation to them is an act of imitation of the pagans and polytheists and it is the worst form of *Shirk*. It is therefore a bounden duty that they keep away from such actions and also advise their brethren regarding it. Relationships of marriage are not admissible with those people who are known to indulge in polytheistic actions; it is also not permissible to eat from their offerings nor to pray for them or behind them until they repent to Allah the All-Mighty and invoke and worship Allah only. Invocation (*Du'â*) is worship; it is indeed the essence of worship. The Prophet صلى الله عليه وسلم has said:

«الدُّعَاءُ هُوَ الْعِبَادَةُ»

"*Du'â* is worship"

and according to another version:

«الدُّعَاءُ مُخُّ الْعِبَادَةِ»

"*Du'â* is the core and essence of worship."

34

Allah the All-Mighty says:

﴿ وَلَا نَنكِحُوا۟ ٱلْمُشْرِكَٰتِ حَتَّىٰ يُؤْمِنَّ وَلَأَمَةٌ مُّؤْمِنَةٌ خَيْرٌ مِّن مُّشْرِكَةٍ وَلَوْ أَعْجَبَتْكُمْ وَلَا تُنكِحُوا۟ ٱلْمُشْرِكِينَ حَتَّىٰ يُؤْمِنُوا۟ وَلَعَبْدٌ مُّؤْمِنٌ خَيْرٌ مِّن مُّشْرِكٍ وَلَوْ أَعْجَبَكُمْ أُو۟لَٰٓئِكَ يَدْعُونَ إِلَى ٱلنَّارِ وَٱللَّهُ يَدْعُوٓا۟ إِلَى ٱلْجَنَّةِ وَٱلْمَغْفِرَةِ بِإِذْنِهِۦ وَيُبَيِّنُ ءَايَٰتِهِۦ لِلنَّاسِ لَعَلَّهُمْ يَتَذَكَّرُونَ ﴾

"And do not marry *Al-Mushrikât* (idolatresses etc.) till they believe (worship Allah Alone). And indeed a slave woman who believes is better than a (free) *Mushrikah* (idolatress etc.), even though she pleases you. And give not (your daughters) in marriage to *Al-Mushrikûn* till they believe (in Allah Alone) and verily, a believing slave is better than a (free) *Mushrik* (idolater etc.), even though he pleases you. Those (*Al-Mushrikûn*) invite you to the Fire, but Allah invites (you) to Paradise and Forgiveness by His Leave, and makes His *Ayât* (proofs, evidences, verses, lessons, signs, revelations, etc.) clear to mankind that they may remember." (V.2:221).

Allah has forbidden Muslims from marrying disbelieving women; such women who worship idols, jinns and angels etc.; marriage is permissible with them only if they sincerely believe in and worship Allah, the One and Only Allah and accept the Message conveyed by the Prophet صلى الله عليه وسلم and proceed on the path shown by him. Allah has also forbidden the marriage of Muslim women to disbelievers until they sincerely believe in Allah and worship Him only and accept the Message conveyed by the Prophet صلى الله عليه وسلم. The Noble Qur'ân states that:

﴿ وَلَأَمَةٌ مُّؤْمِنَةٌ خَيْرٌ مِّن مُّشْرِكَةٍ وَلَوْ أَعْجَبَتْكُمْ ﴾

35

"A slave woman who believes is better than a disbelieving woman, even though she allures you."

and that a man slave who believes is better than a disbeliever, even though he allures you, with his eloquence of speech, courage and chivalry, etc. Allah has then explained the causes for this preference over them by saying that they beckon you to the Fire because they belong to the Fire through their words, actions, manners, conduct and character. As regards the believers — men and women — they are the ones who beckon you to the Paradise through their character, conduct, words and deeds. So, how could the former be equal to the latter? And with regard to the hypocrites Allah the All-Mighty says:

﴿ وَلَا تُصَلِّ عَلَىٰٓ أَحَدٍ مِّنْهُم مَّاتَ أَبَدًا وَلَا تَقُمْ عَلَىٰ قَبْرِهِۦٓ إِنَّهُمْ كَفَرُواْ بِٱللَّهِ وَرَسُولِهِۦ وَمَاتُواْ وَهُمْ فَٰسِقُونَ ﴾

"And never (O Muhammad صلى الله عليه وسلم) pray (funeral prayer) for any of them (hypocrites) who dies, nor stand at his grave. Certainly they disbelieved in Allah and His Messenger, and died while they were *Fâsiqûn* (rebellious — disobedient to Allah and His Messenger)." (V.9:84)

In the above verse, Allah the All-Mighty has stated that one should not offer prayers to the hypocrite and the disbeliever because of their disbelief in Allah and in His Prophet. One should also not pray behind them nor make them as the *Imâm* of Muslims due to their disbelief and untrustworthiness and also due to the great animosity between them and the Muslims; yet another reason is that they are not from the people who pray and worship Allah; heresy and polytheism obliterate all actions. May Allah guard us from such actions. Allah the All-Mighty says in the context of forbidding Muslims from eating the offerings of the disbelievers and dead animals:

﴿ وَلَا تَأْكُلُواْ مِمَّا لَمْ يُذْكَرِ ٱسْمُ ٱللَّهِ عَلَيْهِ وَإِنَّهُۥ لَفِسْقٌ وَإِنَّ ٱلشَّيَٰطِينَ لَيُوحُونَ إِلَىٰٓ أَوْلِيَآئِهِمْ لِيُجَٰدِلُوكُمْ وَإِنْ أَطَعْتُمُوهُمْ إِنَّكُمْ لَمُشْرِكُونَ ﴾

"Eat not (O believers) of that (meat) on which Allah's Name has not been pronounced (at the time of the slaughtering of the animal), for sure it is *Fisq* (a sin and disobedience of Allah). And certainly, the devils do inspire their friends (from mankind) to dispute with you, and if you obey them [by making *Al-Maytata* (a dead animal) legal by eating it], then you would indeed be *Mushrikûn* (polytheists): [because they (devils and their friends) made lawful to you to eat that which Allah has made unlawful to eat and you obeyed them by considering it lawful to eat, and by doing so you worshipped them, and to worship others besides Allah is polytheism]." (V.6:121).

Allah the All-Mighty has forbidden the Muslims from eating dead animals and the animals sacrificed by the disbelievers because the sacrifices given by them are in the category of dead animals, although the Name of Allah may be mentioned; but such mentioning will have no effect for the reason that it is an invocation marred by belief in polytheism; so it cannot be accepted until the polytheist repents to Allah. Allah has permitted the consumption of food offered by the people of the Book (Scripture):

﴿ وَطَعَامُ ٱلَّذِينَ أُوتُواْ ٱلْكِتَٰبَ حِلٌّ لَّكُمْ وَطَعَامُكُمْ حِلٌّ لَّهُمْ ﴾

"The food (slaughtered cattle, eatable animals, etc.) of the people of the Scripture (Jews and Christians) is lawful to you and yours is lawful to them." (V.5:5).

It is lawful because the people of the Book (Scripture) belong to a heavenly religion and claim to be the followers of Moses and Jesus, although this is a false claim. Allah has abrogated their religion and annulled by sending Muhammad صلى الله عليه وسلم as Messenger to all the peoples. However, Allah the All-Mighty has permitted us to accept the food of the people of the Book and to marry their women. The Divine sanction in this regard is due to certain considerations that have been explained by the Scholars. But such a sanction has not been granted with regard to the disbelievers and the polytheists who worship idols, dead people, Prophets, friends and protectors and others because whatever faith they profess is not based on any principle. In fact, all their professions of faith are total falsehoods; therefore, the animals slaughtered by them are dead animals and eating of it is not permissible.

As regards phrases used by people at times of anger such as 'May the jinn strike you'; 'May the jinn take you'; and 'May the jinn fly away with you' are phrases of abuse that are not permissible for the Muslims like all other phrases of abuse and curse, etc. This is not connected with polytheism. However, if the person uttering such words believes that the jinns have a sway over the affairs of the people without the permission of Allah and His will, he will be a disbeliever because Allah the All-Mighty is the Supreme Possessor and Disposer of everything; it is He Who bestows good or causes harm; nothing exists without His permission, His will and His pre-destined plan; Allah has ordered His Prophet to convey to the people:

﴿ قُل لَّآ أَمۡلِكُ لِنَفۡسِى نَفۡعًا وَلَا ضَرًّا إِلَّا مَا شَآءَ ٱللَّهُ وَلَوۡ كُنتُ أَعۡلَمُ ٱلۡغَيۡبَ لَٱسۡتَكۡثَرۡتُ مِنَ ٱلۡخَيۡرِ وَمَا مَسَّنِيَ ٱلسُّوٓءُ إِنۡ أَنَا۠ إِلَّا نَذِيرٌ وَبَشِيرٌ لِّقَوۡمٍ يُؤۡمِنُونَ ﴾

"Say (O Muhammad صلى الله عليه وسلم): I possess no power of benefit or hurt to myself except as Allah wills. If I had the knowledge of the *Ghaib* (unseen), I should have secured for myself an abundance of wealth, and no evil should have touched me. I am but a warner, and a bringer of glad tidings unto people who believe." (V.7:188).

If the leader of all mankind and the best of them, our Prophet صلى الله عليه وسلم does not possess any good nor any harm for himself except what is willed by Allah, how could any other human being do so? There are numerous verses in the Noble Qur'ân in this context.

As regards consulting the soothsayers, magicians, astrologers and others of their tribe who try to predict the unknown, it is a reprehensible act; to believe in them is more reprehensible and objectionable and it is a form of blasphemy because the Prophet صلى الله عليه وسلم has said:

«مَنْ أَتَى عَرَّافًا فَسَأَلَهُ عَنْ شَيْءٍ لَمْ تُقْبَلْ لَهُ صَلَوَاةُ أَرْبَعِينَ يَوْمًا»

"The prayers of a person who consults a soothsayer about anything, will not be accepted for forty days". (Narrated in the *Sahih* of Muslim).

It is also narrated on the authority of Mu'awiyah bin Al-Hakam As-Salami that the Prophet صلى الله عليه وسلم

39

prohibited consultation with soothsayers. It is narrated —
as transmitted by the compilers of *As-Sunan* — that the
Prophet صلى الله عليه وسلم said:

«مَنْ أَتَى كَاهِنًا فَصَدَّقَهُ بِمَا يَقُوْلُ فَقَدْ كَفَرَ بِمَا أُنْزِلَ عَلَى
مُحَمَّدٍ ﷺ»

"He who believes in what a soothsayer says
becomes a disbeliever in what has been revealed to
Muhammad صلى الله عليه وسلم."

There are several sayings of the Prophet in this context.
Muslims therefore, should be on their guard against
soothsayers, sorcerers and witchdoctors who claim
knowledge of the unseen and deceive Muslims on the
pretext of medical treatment or any other excuse. Muslims
should beware of such people as forbidden and cautioned
by the Prophet صلى الله عليه وسلم. In this category, is also
included the claims of some people of knowledge of the
unseen in the name of medicine; they claim knowledge of
the condition of a sick person by smelling his turban or the
veil in case of a woman and so on. In fact, such people
seek only to deceive and confuse the minds of the innocent
people so that they describe him as a person well-informed
in medicine and in treating of illnesses; such a person may
dispense some medicine which may perhaps cure the sick
person; the cure is by the Will of Allah — but the sick
person believes that he was cured because of that
medicine. It is quite possible that the illness is caused by
some of the jinns and evil spirits which are in the employ
of that person who claims himself the knowledge of
medicine, and they provide him with knowledge of the
unseen which they are able to perceive. On the basis of
that knowledge the impostor performs certain worships in
order to please the jinns and the evil spirits so that they

may withdraw from the sick persons. But they invariably leave behind certain harmful effects. This is something well-known about the jinns and evil spirits and those who employ them.

It is therefore, the duty of the Muslims to be on their guard against the above and they should advise each other to abstain from such beliefs and practices and to rely and depend on Allah only on all matters. However, it is not objectionable to use *Ruqya* (recitation of some Divine verses as a treatment for a disease) and the permissible medicines and treatment given by doctors on the basis of physical examination and ascertainment of the physical and mental causes of the illness. The Prophet صلى الله عليه وسلم has said:

«مَا أَنْزَلَ اللهُ دَاءً إِلاَّ أَنْزَلَ لَهُ شِفَاءً عَلِمَهُ مَنْ عَلِمَهُ وَجَهِلَهُ مَنْ جَهِلَهُ»

"Allah has created no disease for which there is no treatment; those who have studied it, know it and those who have ignored it do not know it."

He has also said:

«لِكُلِّ دَاءٍ دَوَاءٌ فَإِذَا أُصِيْبَ دَوَاءُ الدَّاءَ بَرِىءَ بِإِذْنِ اللهِ»

"Every disease has a medicine and if the right medicine is chosen for the disease, the sick person will be cured, Allah willing."

and

«عِبَادَ اللهِ تَدَاوَوْا وَلاَ تَدَاوَوْا بِحَرَامٍ»

"O servants of Allah, take medicines but do not take medicines that are forbidden."

There are many such sayings of the Prophet on this

41

subject. We pray to Allah the All-Mighty to reform all of us Muslims and to cure our minds and bodies from all evils.

May He guide us all to the right path and protect us from evil temptations and from obedience to the Satan and its friends and protectors. Verily, Allah has supreme power over everything; there is no power nor any strength except with Allah, the All-Knowing; and peace and blessings be upon the Prophet of Allah and his Family members and Companions.

In the Name of Allah, the Most Beneficent, the Most Merciful

THE THIRD ESSAY
The Regulation regarding worship through certain innovations which are derived from heretical and polytheistic beliefs

From 'Abdul 'Aziz bin Abdullah bin Baz to Mr.....

May Allah grant him success in everything good. *Amin.* May peace, mercy and blessings of Allah be upon you.

I am in receipt of your letter regarding certain worships at specified times of the day or night practised privately by Muslims of your country. These are prayers to which Allah has not granted any power; among these prayers are those that have been introduced as innovations and those that are polytheistic; they attribute such prayers to the Commander of the Faithful, 'Ali bin Abi Tâlib رضى الله عنه and to others. They recite these prayers in congregations of *Dhikr* (remembrance of Allah) or in the mosques after the *Maghrib* (sunset) prayers in the belief that such prayers will take them nearer to Allah. During these prayers, they utter phrases such as, 'O men of Allah, help us with the Help of Allah and be of succour to us.' They also say, 'O you leaders of authority, O you masters, please respond to our prayers, O you, who possess all help; please intercede with Allah on behalf of this slave who is pleading to you at your door, seized by the fear of his failings; help us O Prophet of Allah; I do not have anyone else to whom I can plead; it is you through whom our wishes can be fulfilled; you are the best of the people of Allah like Hamza, the leader of all martyrs; no one other than you can help us; O Prophet of Allah, come to our help.' They also say, 'O

43

Allah, bless the one you have made as a means for revealing your mighty secrets and your Divine light; he became a true vicegerent and inheritor of all Your Truth.'

You had also desired to know in your letter regarding *Bid'ah* (innovation) and polytheism. You had wanted to know whether it will be correct to pray behind the *Imâm* who makes such invocations.

In this connection, I would like to state the following: -

Praise is to Allah Alone and peace and blessings on the Prophet — the last of all Prophets — and on the members of his Family, his Companions and all those who shall until the Day of Judgement, proceed on the right path shown by him.

Verily, Allah the All-Mighty created the mankind and sent the Messengers عليهم السلام in order that He Alone be worshipped. Allah states in the Noble Qur'ân:

$$ ﴿ وَمَا خَلَقْتُ ٱلْجِنَّ وَٱلْإِنسَ إِلَّا لِيَعْبُدُونِ ﴾ $$

"And I (Allah) created not the jinns and men except they should worship Me (Alone)." (V.51:56)

To worship means to obey the All-Mighty and the Prophet صلى الله عليه وسلم by carrying out what Allah and His Prophet have ordered us to do and by abstaining from what they have forbidden us to do. We carry out these actions with faith, humility and sincere devotion to Allah and His Prophet صلى الله عليه وسلم. The Noble Qur'ân states:

$$ ﴿ وَقَضَىٰ رَبُّكَ أَلَّا تَعْبُدُوٓاْ إِلَّآ إِيَّاهُ ﴾ $$

"And your Lord has decreed that you worship none but Him... (V.17:23)

In other words, He has ordained that He Alone be

worshipped. Allah says in the Noble Qur'ân:

﴿ ٱلۡحَمۡدُ لِلَّهِ رَبِّ ٱلۡعَٰلَمِينَ ٠ ٱلرَّحۡمَٰنِ ٱلرَّحِيمِ ٠ مَٰلِكِ
يَوۡمِ ٱلدِّينِ ٠ إِيَّاكَ نَعۡبُدُ وَإِيَّاكَ نَسۡتَعِينُ ﴾

"All the praises and thanks be to Allah, the Lord of the 'Âlamîn (mankind, jinns and all that exists). The Most Beneficent, the Most Merciful. The Only Owner (and the Only Ruling Judge) of the Day of Recompense (i.e. the Day of Resurrection). You (Alone) we worship, and You (Alone) we ask for help (for each and everything)." (V.1:2-5).

These verses make it amply clear that Allah Alone is to be worshipped and His Help alone is to be sought. Allah also says:

﴿ فَٱعۡبُدِ ٱللَّهَ مُخۡلِصًا لَّهُ ٱلدِّينَ ٠ أَلَا لِلَّهِ ٱلدِّينُ ٱلۡخَالِصُ ﴾

"... So worship Allah (Alone) by doing religious deeds sincerely for Allah's sake only, and not to show off, and not to set up rivals with Him in worship. Surely, the religion (i.e. the worship and the obedience) is for Allah only..." (V.39:2,3)

and

﴿ فَٱدۡعُوا۟ ٱللَّهَ مُخۡلِصِينَ لَهُ ٱلدِّينَ وَلَوۡ كَرِهَ ٱلۡكَٰفِرُونَ ﴾

"So, call you (O Muhammad صلى الله عليه وسلم and the believers) upon (or invoke) Allah making (your) worship pure for Him (Alone) (by worshipping none but Him and by doing religious deeds sincerely for Allah's sake only and not to show off and not to set up rivals with Him in worship). However much the disbelievers (in the Oneness of Allah) may hate (it)." (V.40:14).

and

$$﴿ وَأَنَّ ٱلْمَسَٰجِدَ لِلَّهِ فَلَا تَدْعُوا۟ مَعَ ٱللَّهِ أَحَدًا ﴾$$

"And the mosques are for Allah (Alone), so invoke not anyone along with Allah." (V.72:18).

There are several verses in the Noble Qur'ân in this context pointing out the necessity and the duty to worship Allah Alone. Invocation, as you all know, is, in all its forms, a manner of worship; it is therefore not permissible for anybody to invoke anyone and to seek the help of anyone nor plead for assistance from anyone except Allah, as stated in the above verses. However, in matters pertaining to the daily routine of life and in connection with material things on which every human being has control, a person may seek the help of another person; this is not worship; a person may for example, seek the help of another in order to ward off some evil that may occur to his son or servant or to his dog etc.; one may for example ask for help from his colleague either directly or by correspondence to attend to the building of his house or repairing of his motor car. In this context, Allah the All-Mighty says while narrating the story of the Prophet Moses (Mûsa) عليه السلام :

$$﴿ فَٱسْتَغَٰثَهُ ٱلَّذِى مِن شِيعَتِهِۦ عَلَى ٱلَّذِى مِنْ عَدُوِّهِۦ ﴾$$

"...The man of his (own) party asked him for help against his foe..." (V.28:15).

The help and aid which a man seeks from his fellow human beings at times of *Jihâd* (fighting the disbelievers) and conflict is like the above said help. But seeking help and aid from the dead, the jinns, the angels, the trees and the stones is an act of major polytheism; it is similar to the practices of the polytheists of the early ages with their gods such as *Al-'Uzza* and *Al-Laat,* etc. Similarly, it is an

46

act of polytheism to believe that certain human beings enjoy or possess certain supernatural powers which belong only to Allah the All-Mighty. It is believed that such people can help in curing the sick, showing the path of right guidance to those who go astray, attaining the Paradise and salvation from the Hell. The verses quoted above and the sayings of the Prophet referred to, emphasize the need to guide all people to the path of Allah in all matters and to be sincere in worshipping Allah and Allah Only because all human beings have been created for that purpose and have been thus ordained as mentioned in the verses quoted above. Allah the All-Mighty also says:

$$ ﴿ وَٱعْبُدُوا۟ ٱللَّهَ وَلَا تُشْرِكُوا۟ بِهِۦ شَيْـًٔا ﴾ $$

"Worship Allah and join none with Him in worship..." (V.4:36).

and

$$ ﴿ وَمَآ أُمِرُوٓا۟ إِلَّا لِيَعْبُدُوا۟ ٱللَّهَ مُخْلِصِينَ لَهُ ٱلدِّينَ حُنَفَآءَ ﴾ $$

"And they were commanded not, but that they should worship Allah, and worship none but Him Alone (abstaining from ascribing partners to Him)..." (V.98:5)

and the Prophet صلى الله عليه وسلم has said as narrated by Mu'âdh رضى الله عنه:

$$ «حَقُّ اللهِ عَلَى الْعِبَادِ أَنْ يَعْبُدُوْهُ وَلَا يُشْرِكُوْا بِهِ شَيْئًا» $$

"It is Allah's Right over the worshippers that they worship only Him and do not associate anyone with Him."

and the Prophet صلى الله عليه وسلم has said in another tradition narrated by Mas'ûd:

$$ «مَنْ مَاتَ وَهُوَ يَدْعُوْ للهِ نِدًّا دَخَلَ النَّارَ» $$

"Whoever dies while invoking someone as rival to Allah, will be doomed to Hell."

This tradition has been narrated by Imam Al-Bukhari. When the Prophet ﷺ sent the Companion Mu'âdh رضي الله عنه to Yemen, he said to him:

«إِنَّكَ تَأْتِي قَوْمًا أَهْلَ كِتَابٍ فَلْيَكُنْ أَوَّلَ مَا تَدْعُوهُمْ إِلَيْهِ شَهَادَةُ أَنْ لاَّ إِلَهَ إِلاَّ اللهُ»

«فَادْعُهُمْ إِلَى أَنْ يَشْهَدُوا أَنْ لاَّ إِلَهَ إِلا اللهُ وَأَنِّي رَسُولُ اللهِ»

"You shall be meeting a people who profess faith in a Revealed Book; therefore, your plea to them should be to profess the Statement of Faith: 'There is no god except Allah and that I (Muhammad) am the Messenger of Allah.' "

In the narration of Imâm Bukhari it is mentioned as:

«فَادْعُهُمْ إِلَى أَنْ يُوَحِّدُوا اللهَ»

"Plead to them until they accept the Oneness of Allah."

It is narrated in the Collection of *Ahâdîth* compiled by Imâm Muslim that according to a saying narrated by Tariq bin Ashyam Al-Ashja'i that the Prophet ﷺ said:

«مَنْ وَحَّدَ اللهَ وَكَفَرَ بِمَا يُعْبَدُ مِنْ دُونِ اللهِ حُرِمَ مَالُهُ وَدَمُهُ وَحِسَابُهُ عَلَى اللهِ عَزَّ وَجَلَّ»

"Whoever accepts the Oneness of Allah and disbelieves whatever is worshipped other than Allah enjoys the protection of Allah in his wealth, blood and his reward is with Allah."

There are numerous *Ahâdîth* (traditions) on this subject.

The Faith in the Oneness of Allah is the sum and substance of the religion of Islâm; It is the basic principle and the most important of all the duties. And it is for this purpose that the human beings and the jinns were created. It was for the same object that the Messengers of Allah عليهم السلام were sent. We had earlier quoted several verses from the Noble Qur'ân affirming this fact. Among such verses are:

$$ ﴿ وَمَا خَلَقْتُ ٱلْجِنَّ وَٱلْإِنسَ إِلَّا لِيَعْبُدُونِ ﴾ $$

"And I (Allah) created not the jinns and men except they should worship Me (Alone)." (V.51:56)

and

$$ ﴿ وَلَقَدْ بَعَثْنَا فِى كُلِّ أُمَّةٍ رَّسُولًا أَنِ ٱعْبُدُواْ ٱللَّهَ وَٱجْتَنِبُواْ ٱلطَّٰغُوتَ ﴾ $$

"And verily, We have sent among every *Ummah* (community, nation) a Messenger (proclaiming): Worship Allah (Alone), and avoid (or keep away from) *Tâghût* (all false deities etc. i.e. do not worship *Tâghûts* besides Allah)." (V.16:36)

and

$$ ﴿ وَمَآ أَرْسَلْنَا مِن قَبْلِكَ مِن رَّسُولٍ إِلَّا نُوحِىٓ إِلَيْهِ أَنَّهُ لَآ إِلَٰهَ إِلَّآ أَنَا۠ فَٱعْبُدُونِ ﴾ $$

"And We did not send any Messenger before you (O Muhammad صلى الله عليه وسلم) but We inspired him (saying): *Lâ ilâha illa Ana* [none has the right to be worshipped but I (Allah)], so worship Me (Alone and none else,)". (V.21:25)

Referring to the Prophets Noah, Hûd, Sâleh and Sho'aib

49

السلام عليهم , Allah the All-Mighty says that these Prophets advised their peoples:

﴿اعْبُدُوا اللَّهَ مَا لَكُم مِّنْ إِلَهٍ غَيْرُهُ﴾

"...O my people! Worship Allah! You have no other *Ilâh* (God) but Him. (*La ilaha ill-Allah*: none has the right to be worshipped but Allah)...." (V.7:59)

This was the Message of all the Prophets. All those who oppose the Prophets have themselves confessed that the Prophets had commanded them to worship Allah Only and to give up the worship of all other gods. The Noble Qur'ân says in this context, referring to the story of 'Âd that they told the Prophet Hûd السلام عليه.:

﴿أَجِئْتَنَا لِنَعْبُدَ اللَّهَ وَحْدَهُ وَنَذَرَ مَا كَانَ يَعْبُدُ ءَابَاؤُنَا﴾

"They said: You have come to us that we should worship Allah Alone and forsake that which our fathers used to worship..." (V.7: 70)

And Allah the All-Mighty says about the people of the tribe of Quraish when they were called upon by our Prophet Muhammad صلى الله عليه وسلم, to worship Allah Only and to give up worshipping the angels, the friends and guides, idols and trees, etc.:

﴿أَجَعَلَ الْآلِهَةَ إِلَهًا وَاحِدًا إِنَّ هَذَا لَشَيْءٌ عُجَابٌ﴾

"Has he made the *âlihâ* (gods) (all) into One *Ilâh* (God — Allah). Verily, this is a curious thing!" (V.38:5)

And in the *Sûrah* (Chapter) *As-Sâffât*, Allah says:

﴿إِنَّهُمْ كَانُوا إِذَا قِيلَ لَهُمْ لَا إِلَهَ إِلَّا اللَّهُ يَسْتَكْبِرُونَ ۝ وَيَقُولُونَ أَئِنَّا لَتَارِكُوا ءَالِهَتِنَا لِشَاعِرٍ مَّجْنُونٍ﴾

50

"Truly, when it was said to them: 'Lâ ilaha ill-Allah (none has the right to be worshipped but Allah),' they puffed themselves up with pride (i.e. denied it). And (they) said: 'Are we going to abandon our âlihâ (gods) for the sake of a mad poet?' " (V.37:35,36)

There are many more verses in the Noble Qur'ân and sayings of the Noble Prophet صلى الله عليه وسلم which expound this concept. May Allah grant success to us all in understanding our religion and in educating ourselves regarding the true path of Allah.

All the invocations and different expressions seeking help and succour are various forms of polytheism because they are addressed as worship to other than Allah; and they seek to achieve things through the dead and the departed whereas Allah Alone can grant those things.

Such invocations are more worse forms of polytheism when compared to the polytheism of the early ages because the people of the early ages indulged in polytheism only when they enjoyed material comfort, peace and luxury. But at times of crisis and hardships they worshipped Allah Alone because they know that Allah Alone can bring salvation to them from their hardships. The Noble Qur'ân refers to those polytheists and says:

﴿ فَإِذَا رَكِبُوا فِى ٱلْفُلْكِ دَعَوُا ٱللَّهَ مُخْلِصِينَ لَهُ ٱلدِّينَ فَلَمَّا نَجَّىٰهُمْ إِلَى ٱلْبَرِّ إِذَا هُمْ يُشْرِكُونَ ﴾

"And when they embark on a ship, they invoke Allah, making their Faith pure for Him only, but when He brings them safely to land, behold, they give a share of their worship to others." (V.29:65) and Allah says in another verse:

﴿ وَإِذَا مَسَّكُمُ ٱلضُّرُّ فِى ٱلْبَحْرِ ضَلَّ مَن تَدْعُونَ إِلَّآ إِيَّاهُ فَلَمَّا نَجَّىٰكُمْ إِلَى ٱلْبَرِّ أَعْرَضْتُمْ وَكَانَ ٱلْإِنسَٰنُ كَفُورًا ﴾

"And when harm touches you upon the sea, those that you call upon besides Him vanish from you except Him (Allah Alone). But when He brings you safely to land, you turn away (from Him). And man is ever ungrateful." (V.17:67)

If the latter-day polytheists were to say, "We do not mean that those whose help we seek can by themselves benefit us and cure the sick among us or be of use to us or hurt us; we only mean to seek their intercession with Allah for us, the answer to such an observation should be as follows:

Verily, the disbelievers of the early period also had the same purpose and desire; they too did not believe that their gods create or give livelihood or do good or harm.

Such a statement will negate what Allah has mentioned about them in the Noble Qur'ân. Those disbelievers also claimed that they only sought, through such worship, the intercession and good offices of those whom they worshipped so that they may take them nearer to Allah. Allah says in the Noble Qur'ân in the context of the story of the Prophet Yûnus عليه السلام.:

﴿ وَيَعْبُدُونَ مِن دُونِ ٱللَّهِ مَا لَا يَضُرُّهُمْ وَلَا يَنفَعُهُمْ وَيَقُولُونَ هَٰٓؤُلَآءِ شُفَعَٰٓؤُنَا عِندَ ٱللَّهِ قُلْ أَتُنَبِّئُونَ ٱللَّهَ بِمَا لَا يَعْلَمُ فِى ٱلسَّمَٰوَٰتِ وَلَا فِى ٱلْأَرْضِ سُبْحَٰنَهُ وَتَعَٰلَىٰ عَمَّا يُشْرِكُونَ ﴾

"And they worship besides Allah things that hurt them not, nor profit them, and they say: 'These are our intercessors with Allah.' Say: 'Do you inform Allah of that which He knows not in the heavens and on the earth?' Glorified and Exalted be He above all that which they associate as partners with Him!" (V.10:18)

Thus Allah states in unmistakable words that He has no knowledge of any intercessor from the heavens or from the earth as claimed by the disbelievers. So, the existence of anything not known to Allah does not in fact exist because nothing is hidden from His Knowledge. Allah says in the Noble Qur'ân:

﴿تَنزِيلُ ٱلْكِتَـٰبِ مِنَ ٱللَّهِ ٱلْعَزِيزِ ٱلْحَكِيمِ ○ إِنَّا أَنزَلْنَآ إِلَيْكَ ٱلْكِتَـٰبَ بِٱلْحَقِّ فَٱعْبُدِ ٱللَّهَ مُخْلِصًا لَّهُ ٱلدِّينَ ○ أَلَا لِلَّهِ ٱلدِّينُ ٱلْخَالِصُ﴾

"The revelation of this Book (the Qur'ân) is from Allah, the All-Mighty, the All-Wise. Verily, We have sent down the Book to you (O Muhammad صلى الله عليه وسلم) in Truth. So worship Allah (Alone) by doing religious deeds sincerely for Allah's sake only, and not to show off, and not to set up rivals with Him in worship. Surely, the religion (i.e. the worship and the obedience) is for Allah only..." (V.39:1-3).

It is evident from these verses that Allah Alone is to be worshipped and such worship should be in all sincerity because Allah has commanded the Prophet صلى الله عليه وسلم to be sincere in worship. This command applies to all the believers. In the above quoted verse, the word *Ad-Deen* meaning religion in Arabic has been interpreted as worship; worship means obedience to Allah and His Prophet صلى الله عليه وسلم as stated earlier; it includes invocation, seeking help, fear, hope, vows and sacrifices besides

53

prayers and fasting and other duties as ordained by Allah and His Prophet صلى الله عليه وسلم. Later on, Allah says in the Noble Qur'ân:

﴿ وَٱلَّذِينَ ٱتَّخَذُوا۟ مِن دُونِهِۦٓ أَوْلِيَآءَ مَا نَعْبُدُهُمْ إِلَّا لِيُقَرِّبُونَآ إِلَى ٱللَّهِ زُلْفَىٰٓ ﴾

"...And those who take 'Auliyâ' (protectors and helpers) besides Him (say): We worship them only that they may bring us near to Allah...." (V.39:3)

In other words, they sought to say that their only purpose was to achieve nearness to Allah. In answer to this, Allah says:

﴿ إِنَّ ٱللَّهَ يَحْكُمُ بَيْنَهُمْ فِى مَا هُمْ فِيهِ يَخْتَلِفُونَ إِنَّ ٱللَّهَ لَا يَهْدِى مَنْ هُوَ كَٰذِبٌ كَفَّارٌ ﴾

"...Verily, Allah will judge between them concerning that wherein they differ. Truly, Allah guides not him who is a liar, and a disbeliever." (V.39:3).

Thus the falsehood of their claim that their gods take them nearer to Allah has been exposed and the worship they perform has been described as blasphemy. It should therefore be clear to any person who has even a minimum of intelligence that the source of blasphemy and polytheism in the earlier ages was because Prophets, friends and advisors besides trees and stones and other creations were considered intercessors between the worshippers and Allah, and they believed that such intercessors achieve for them their hopes and aspirations, needs and ambitions without the Permission nor the Consent of Allah the All-Mighty. It was considered to be like the recommendation of the ministers to the kings and they (such worshippers) presumed Allah, the All-Mighty to be equal to kings and leaders and therefore, they uttered words which one may utter when making a petition to a king or a leader. This is the worst form of falsehood because Allah the All-Mighty has none similar to Him and He cannot be compared with His Own creations; no one intercedes with Him without His Permission; intercession is granted only to the believers in the Oneness of Allah; Allah is Omnipotent and Omniscient and He is Most Merciful; He does not fear anyone and neither can anyone frighten Him since He has power over all His servants and He Alone disposes their affairs as He wills. On the contrary, kings and leaders cannot have power over anything and they do not have knowledge about everything. So they need to have people to assist them in matters which they are unable to achieve or implement. Hence, they are always surrounded by an entourage of ministers, advisers and bodyguards, etc. They also need to be informed about those who are in want; this is yet another reason for their being surrounded by ministers and advisers. But Allah the All-Mighty is above all such needs and all such assistance. He is more merciful to them than their mothers; and He is the Just Ruler, Who as per His Supreme Knowledge, Wisdom and Ability assigns everything to its proper place; it is therefore not permissible to compare Him with His Own creations. It is for this reason that Allah the All-Mighty has stated in the Noble Qur'ân that He is the Creator and the Sustainer; it is He Who responds to the call of one who is in distress and exposes the evil, gives life and takes it away; and does so many other actions. The dispute between the polytheists and the Messengers of Allah is in fact about the sincerity in worshipping Allah Alone. The Noble Qur'ân says:

﴿ وَلَئِن سَأَلْتَهُم مَّنْ خَلَقَهُمْ لَيَقُولُنَّ ٱللَّهُ ﴾

"And if you ask them who created them, they will surely say: Allah..." (V.43:87).

﴿ قُلْ مَن يَرْزُقُكُم مِّنَ ٱلسَّمَآءِ وَٱلْأَرْضِ أَمَّن يَمْلِكُ ٱلسَّمْعَ وَٱلْأَبْصَـٰرَ وَمَن يُخْرِجُ ٱلْحَىَّ مِنَ ٱلْمَيِّتِ وَيُخْرِجُ ٱلْمَيِّتَ مِنَ ٱلْحَىِّ وَمَن يُدَبِّرُ ٱلْأَمْرَ فَسَيَقُولُونَ ٱللَّهُ فَقُلْ أَفَلَا تَتَّقُونَ ﴾

"Say: 'Who provides for you from the sky and from the earth? Or who owns hearing and sight? And who brings out the living from the dead and brings out the dead from the living? And who disposes the affairs?' They will say: 'Allah.' Say: 'Will you not then be afraid of Allah's Punishment (for setting up rivals in worship with Allah)?' " (V.10:31).

There are several verses in this context in the Noble Qur'ân. We had earlier referred to the verses that point out that the dispute, between the Messengers of Allah and the nations, was regarding sincerity in worshipping alone. We may quote another verse:

﴿ وَلَقَدْ بَعَثْنَا فِى كُلِّ أُمَّةٍ رَّسُولًا أَنِ ٱعْبُدُوا۟ ٱللَّهَ وَٱجْتَنِبُوا۟ ٱلطَّـٰغُوتَ ﴾

"And verily, We have sent among every *Ummah* (community, nation) a Messenger (proclaiming): Worship Allah (Alone), and avoid (or keep away from) *Tâghût* (all false deities etc. i.e. do not worship *Tâghûts* besides Allah)."... (V.16:36)

Regarding intercession, Allah the All-Mighty has mentioned in several places in the Noble Qur'ân, the real meaning of intercession. We may for example quote:

﴿ مَن ذَا ٱلَّذِى يَشْفَعُ عِندَهُۥٓ إِلَّا بِإِذْنِهِۦ ﴾

56

"...Who is he that can intercede with Him except with His Permission?...." (V.2:255).

Allah will not accept from His worshippers blasphemy heathenism; He will accept only gratitude expressed by the belief in the Oneness of Allah and obedience to Him. It is stated in the Noble Qur'ân:

﴿وَكَم مِّن مَّلَكٍ فِي ٱلسَّمَٰوَٰتِ لَا تُغْنِى شَفَٰعَتُهُمْ شَيْئًا إِلَّا مِنۢ بَعْدِ أَن يَأْذَنَ ٱللَّهُ لِمَن يَشَآءُ وَيَرْضَىٰٓ﴾

" And there are many angels in the heavens, whose intercession will avail nothing except after Allah has given leave for whom He wills and pleases."(V.53:26)

and

﴿وَلَا يَشْفَعُونَ إِلَّا لِمَنِ ٱرْتَضَىٰ وَهُم مِّنْ خَشْيَتِهِۦ مُشْفِقُونَ﴾

"...and they cannot intercede except for him with whom He is pleased. And they stand in awe for fear of Him." (V.21:28)

and

﴿إِن تَكْفُرُوا۟ فَإِنَّ ٱللَّهَ غَنِىٌّ عَنكُمْ وَلَا يَرْضَىٰ لِعِبَادِهِ ٱلْكُفْرَ وَإِن تَشْكُرُوا۟ يَرْضَهُ لَكُمْ﴾

"If you disbelieve, then verily, Allah is not in need of you, He likes not disbelief for His slaves. And if you are grateful (by being believers), He is pleased therewith for you..." (V.39:7)

It is narrated in the Collections of Traditions (Ahâdith) compiled by Imâm Bukharî that Abû Huraira رضى الله عنه said that when he asked the Prophet صلى الله عليه وسلم :

"Who shall be the most happy people with your

57

intercession, O Prophet of Allah?" The Prophet said:

«مَنْ قَالَ لاَ إِلَهَ إِلاَّ اللهُ خَالِصًا مِن قَلْبِهِ»

"He who says that there is no god except Allah, and says so with all the sincerity of his heart (or of his self)."

It is narrated on the authority of Anas رضى الله عنه that the Prophet صلى الله عليه وسلم said:

«لِكُلِّ نَبِيٍّ دَعْوَةٌ مُسْتَجَابَةٌ فَتَعَجَّلَ كُلُّ نَبِيٍّ دَعْوَتَهُ وَأَنِّي اخْتَبَأْتُ دَعْوَتِي شَفَاعَةً لِأُمَّتِي يَوْمَ الْقِيَامَةِ فَهِيَ نَائِلَةٌ إِنْ شَاءَ اللهُ مَنْ مَاتَ مِنْ أُمَّتِي لاَ يُشْرِكُ بِاللهِ شَيْئًا»

"Every Prophet has a plea responded to; and every Prophet hastened to make his plea while I withheld mine, so that I may intercede for my *Ummah* (nation) on the Day of the Judgement; and by the Will of Allah my intercession will include all of my *Ummah* who have departed from this world without setting up partners to Allah in worship."

There are several verses in the Noble Qur'ân and several *Ahâdith* (traditions) of the Prophet which emphasize the fact that worship is a right preserved for Allah Alone and it is not permissible to perform any worship to anyone other than Allah, whether they be the Prophets or any other person. They also emphasize the fact that intercession is with Allah the All-Mighty Alone as said in the Noble Qur'ân:

﴿قُل لِّلَّهِ الشَّفَٰعَةُ جَمِيعًا﴾

"Say: To Allah belongs all intercession..." (V.39:44).

No one shall deserve the intercession except by His Permission. And He, the All-Mighty, will permit for intercession to persons who only believe in the Oneness of Allah as stated earlier. Therefore, the polytheists will not be granted intercession. The Noble Qur'ân says:

$$﴿ فَمَا تَنفَعُهُمْ شَفَاعَةُ ٱلشَّافِعِينَ ﴾$$

"So no intercession of intercessors will be of any use to them." (V.74:48)

$$﴿ مَا لِلظَّالِمِينَ مِنْ حَمِيمٍ وَلَا شَفِيعٍ يُطَاعُ ﴾$$

"... There will be no friend, nor an intercessor for the *Zâlimûn* (polytheists and the wrong-doers, etc.), who could be given heed to." (V.40:18)

The expression '*Zâlimun* (wrong-doers)' in this verse is interpreted as the polytheists; this is stated in another verse:

$$﴿ وَٱلْكَٰفِرُونَ هُمُ ٱلظَّٰلِمُونَ ﴾$$

"...And it is the disbelievers who are the *Zâlimûn* (wrong-doers, etc.). (V.2:254)

$$﴿ إِنَّ ٱلشِّرْكَ لَظُلْمٌ عَظِيمٌ ﴾$$

"...Verily! Joining others in worship with Allah is a great *Zûlm* (wrong) indeed." (V.31:13)

With regard to your question concerning some of the *Sufis* (mystics) who utter in the mosques and in some other places phrases such as 'O Lord, grant peace and blessings on the one whom you have ordained to be instrumental in the unfolding of Your Mighty Secrets and in opening the doors to the sublime lights of Your Mercy and who has thus become Your vicegerent and who has inherited Your Hidden Secrets... etc.' The answer to this would be:

All such utterances are nothing but pedantry and empty

talk against which our Prophet Muhammad صلى الله عليه وسلم has warned us. It is narrated in the Collection of Traditions (*Ahâdîth*) by Imâm Muslim on the authority of 'Abdullah bin Masûd رضى الله عنه that the Prophet صلى الله عليه وسلم said:

$$ «هَلَكَ الْمُتَنَطِّعُوْنَ» $$

"The pedants shall be doomed to destruction."

(The Prophet صلى الله عليه وسلم repeated this remark three times).

Imâm Al-Khattabi رحمه الله has defined a pedant as one who delves into problems and issues which are beyond his intellectual abilities, as was indulged by the scholastic theologians.

Abus-Sa'âdât Ibn-al-Athir has said that the pedants are those who show extravagance in their speech and try to speak too loudly. The Arabic word for this expression *Mutanatti'* is derived from *Nat'* meaning forepart of the palate. Later, the word was used for every extravagant either in speech or action.

Any person, even with a minimum of intelligence, will understand from the above that such utterances referred to, in praise of our Prophet صلى الله عليه وسلم , is a form of affectation and pedantry forbidden in our religion. The correct approach for a Muslim in this context should be to learn the Traditional method of sending *Salât* (blessing) on the Prophet صلى الله عليه وسلم Imâm Bukhari and Imâm Muslim have narrated in their Collections on the authority of Ka'b bin 'Ujrah رضى الله عنه that the Companions of the Prophet رضى الله عنهم said to the Prophet صلى الله عليه وسلم: O Prophet of Allah, we have been ordered to send *Salât* (blessings) on you; how shall we send *Salât* (blessing) on you?" The Prophet said:

$$ «اللّٰهُمَّ صَلِّ عَلَى مُحَمَّدٍ وَعَلَى آلِ مُحَمَّدٍ كَمَا صَلَّيْتَ عَلَى $$

إِبْرَاهِيمَ وَعَلَى آلِ إِبْرَاهِيمَ إِنَّكَ حَمِيدٌ مَجِيدٌ وَبَارِكْ عَلَى مُحَمَّدٍ وَعَلَى آلِ مُحَمَّدٍ كَمَا بَارَكْتَ عَلَى إِبْرَاهِيمَ وَعَلَى آلِ إِبْرَاهِيمَ إِنَّكَ حَمِيدٌ مَجِيدٌ»

"Say: O Lord, bless Muhammad and the family of Muhammad as You blessed Ibrâhîm and the family of Ibrâhîm; verily You are Praiseworthy and Glorious; and O Lord, grant Your benedictions to Muhammad and the family of Muhammad as You granted to Ibrâhîm and the family of Ibrâhim; verily You are Praiseworthy and Glorious.".

It is also narrated in the Collections of Imâm Bukharî and Imâm Muslim on the authority of Abi Humaid As-Sa'idi رضى الله عنه that some people asked the Prophet صلى الله عليه وسلم:

"How shall we send *Salât* (blessings) on you, O Prophet of Allah?" The Prophet صلى الله عليه وسلم said,

«قُولُوا اللَّهُمَّ صَلِّ عَلَى مُحَمَّدٍ وَعَلَى أَزْوَاجِهِ وَذُرِّيَّتِهِ كَمَا صَلَّيْتَ عَلَى آلِ إِبْرَاهِيمَ وَبَارِكْ عَلَى مُحَمَّدٍ وَأَزْوَاجِهِ وَذُرِّيَّتِهِ كَمَا بَارَكْتَ عَلَى آلِ إِبْرَاهِيمَ إِنَّكَ حَمِيدٌ مَجِيدٌ»

"Say: O Lord, bless Muhammad, his wives and his children as You blessed the family of Ibrâhîm and grant Your benedictions on Muhammad, his wives and his children as You granted to the family of Ibrâhîm. Verily You are Praiseworthy and Glorious."

It is narrated in the Collection of Imâm Muslim on the authority of Abi Mas'ud Al-Ansâri رضى الله عنه that Basheer bin Sa'd رضى الله عنه said:

«قُولُوا اللَّهُمَّ صَلِّ عَلَى مُحَمَّدٍ وَعَلَى آلِ مُحَمَّدٍ كَمَا صَلَّيْتَ عَلَى إِبْرَاهِيمَ وَبَارِكْ عَلَى مُحَمَّدٍ وَعَلَى آلِ مُحَمَّدٍ كَمَا بَارَكْتَ عَلَى إِبْرَاهِيمَ فِي الْعَالَمِينَ إِنَّكَ حَمِيدٌ مَجِيدٌ وَالسَّلَامُ كَمَا عَلِمْتُمْ».

"O Prophet of Allah, Allah has ordered us to send *Salât* (blessing) on you; so how shall we send *Salât* (blessing) on you?" The Prophet remained silent for a few moments and then said, "Say: O Lord, bless Muhammad and the family of Muhammad as You blessed Ibrâhîm and bestow Your benediction on Muhammad and the family of Muhammad as You bestowed on Ibrahim in the two worlds; verily You are Praiseworthy and Glorious. This is the prayer taught to you."

All such utterances that are authentically attributed to the Prophet صلى الله عليه وسلم should be the only utterances used by a Muslim whenever he seeks to pray for the Prophet and ask for Allah's benediction for him. A Muslim should abide only by these authentic words because the Prophet صلى الله عليه وسلم knows best regarding the words that are to be used for him and he also knows best regarding the words that are to be used for his Lord. As regards, all the innovated and affected words and phrases besides the words which are loaded with the possibility of incorrect connotations such as the words mentioned in your query; such words should not be used because they are affected forms of speech and because they can be interpreted with false meanings and also for the reason they are different from the words selected by the Prophet of Allah صلى الله عليه وسلم. He has instructed his *Ummah* (nation) and he is the best informed among all human beings and the most righteous; he is the least inclined to affectations. May the best of peace and blessings from our Lord be on him. I hope that the discussion I have presented in these pages, supported by adequate proofs, shall suffice in explaining the truth of the doctrine of the Oneness of Allah and in exposing polytheism besides explaining the differences between the polytheists of the early ages and those of the later ages in this regard.

A person who seeks to know the truth should be convinced by the explanation given regarding the permissible form of *Salât* (blessings) on the Prophet صلى الله عليه وسلم. But if a person has no desire to know the truth, he can indulge in his own fanciful thoughts. Allah has referred to them in the Noble Qur'ân and said:

﴿ فَإِن لَّمْ يَسْتَجِيبُوا۟ لَكَ فَٱعْلَمْ أَنَّمَا يَتَّبِعُونَ أَهْوَآءَهُمْ وَمَنْ أَضَلُّ مِمَّنِ ٱتَّبَعَ هَوَىٰهُ بِغَيْرِ هُدًى مِّنَ ٱللَّهِ إِنَّ ٱللَّهَ لَا يَهْدِى ٱلْقَوْمَ ٱلظَّٰلِمِينَ ﴾

"But if they answer you not (i.e. do not believe in your doctrine of Islamic Monotheism, nor follow you), then know that they only follow their own lusts. And who is more astray than one who follows his own lusts, without guidance from Allah? Verily! Allah guides not the people who are *Zâlimûn* (wrong-doers, disobedient to Allah, and polytheists)." (V.28:50)

In the above verse Allah the All-Mighty has classified the people in two groups with regard to their attitude to our Prophet Muhammad صلى الله عليه وسلم and his mission; One group responds to Allah and to His Messenger whereas the other group follows its own lusts and Allah says that those who follow their lusts are deprived of all guidance from Him.

We pray to Allah the All-Mighty, that we may be safe from becoming the followers of lusts and may Allah make you and all of us among those who always abide by the path of Allah and His Messenger صلى الله عليه وسلم and by those who enlighten us about his Divine Law (*Shari'a*) and caution us against whatever is in violation of it, such as innovations and fanciful opinions. Verily, Allah is Magnanimous and Generous. Peace and blessings be on His slave and Messenger, our Prophet Muhammad and on his Family, his Companions and his followers until the Day of Judgement.